Golde's Homemade Cookies

A TREASURED COLLECTION OF TIMELESS RECIPES

by Golde Hoffman Soloway

Illustrated by Loretta Trezzo

WILLIAMSON PUBLISHING
CHARLOTTE, VERMONT 05445

Special thanks to Harriet Patrick and Peg Blanchette for their assistance and enthusiastic support in bringing this project to completion.

Library of Congress Cataloging in Publication Data

Soloway, Golde Hoffman.
  Golde's homemade cookies.

  Includes index.
  1. Cookies. I. Title.
TX772.S67 1984 641.8'654 84-22014
ISBN 0-913589-05-5

Cover and interior design: Trezzo-Braren Studio
Illustrations: Loretta Trezzo
Typography: Villanti & Sons, Printers, Inc.
Printing: Capital City Press

Contents

DEDICATION

For David.

ACKNOWLEDGEMENTS

With abundant thanks . . .

To all the wonderful people who have shared recipes with me over these many years.

To my family and friends who have gathered around our table for coffee, tea, cookies and good conversation.

To Susan Williamson for her editorial assistance, to Jack Williamson for his enthusiastic delight in this book, to Loretta Trezzo for her beautiful illustrations and book design.

And to my grandchildren – Rachel, Daniel, Sarah, Zachary, Joelle, and Jonathan.

Introduction

People often ask how I got so involved in cookie-baking. My answer is always the same, uninspired as it might seem; I bake cookies because in the time it takes to bake one cake, I can bake dozens of cookies, and, I must admit, because my pie crusts never quite measure up to my friends' and neighbors'.

My daughters, who are into the psychological meaning of such things, tell me that my cookies are my personal expression of love and caring. And there is some truth to that for cookies were always my way of celebrating the joy of family, friends and neighbors at weddings, Bar Mitzvahs, graduations, holidays, anniversaries, and impromptu get-togethers; in fact, just about any happy occasion. And, too, I find I send cookies to help ease the burden during painful events in the lives of the people close to me.

Then there is this a-little-something-for-the-trip-home habit – I think it started when my eldest daughter went to college – of sending cookies home with house guests. (Invariably, I always hear how the cookies are all gone before they reach their destination.) And, of course, I bring tins of cookies whenever I go off for a visit; now that I know most friends' favorites, I try to take those along, always mixed with something new that I'm trying.

So I guess my daughters are right. Cookies are my way of saying to someone that they are special – right down to their favorite kinds of cookies. And it does give me pleasure to see my family and friends brighten up and say, "Ah, good! Some of Golde's cookies!"

HOMEMADE IS BETTER

In this age of fast food and instant satisfaction, it gets harder and harder to justify some of the time-consuming methods, or as my grandchildren say "olden times" ways of doing things.

Not so, with homebaked cookies. Plain and simply, homebaked cookies *taste* much better than anything you can buy. There is really no comparison with store-bought cookies. Actually, the packaged varieties don't even deserve to be called "cookies", and the only ones I buy are from the Girl Scouts (still the best chocolate cookie mints anywhere). Bakeries in supermarkets and in malls don't really come close to homebaked cookies either.

Actually, I think any cookie should be considered suspect if it is surrounded by perfectly shaped, perfectly browned, perfectly *perfect* identical cookies. Give me a good batch of homemade *individuality* anytime, fresh from the oven, the house filled with the aroma of mingling spices, each cookie slightly different in shape and size. They might not win any blue ribbons at the county fair and they'd never meet bakery standards in appearance, but for flavor, texture, and aroma, they're unbeatable.

FINDING THE TIME TO BAKE

Let's face it . . . free time is a thing of the past. We're all too busy, our calendars filled with meetings, appointments, and varied responsibilities. But, take another look; isn't there a small amount of time here or there, because that's all you really need, a small bit of time.

As you'll see, I've recorded preparation time for all of my recipes, and some need as little as 10-15 minutes to prepare the batter. So do that much and stick the batter in the fridge (covered with plastic wrap) until later that day when you're preparing dinner or the next day when you have another bit of spare time. Then bake that batch or two. There, you've baked some delicious cookies in time that otherwise would have been unproductive.

Basically, *fit your cookie-baking into the rhythm of your lifestyle*, rather than planning your day around cookie-baking time. When you have the time, bake and freeze the extras. When you don't have the time or inclination, dig into your freezer reserve.

I do most of my baking in the wee hours of the morning. If I can't sleep, I get up and make a batch or two. (It's a lot better than worrying about not sleeping.) I feel comfortable padding around the kitchen in the early sunrise hours, and my family loves awakening to the aroma of freshly baked cookies.

Most importantly, think of cookie-baking as part of your leisure time activity – relaxation rather than a chore – fun to do with friends and neighborhood children, and you'll be surprised how quickly time makes itself available.

PLAN WAY AHEAD

If you need a large number of cookies for a particular time of year or a special event, then plan way ahead. I have all of my holiday baking done three months in advance, except for some special cookies that my grandchildren like baking right around holiday time.

I always bake in the late spring so there's a freezer full of cookies for those hot summer days; this way I don't have to heat up the house with a hot oven, and I still have some special treats to go with iced tea or fresh fruit.

For my grandson's Bar Mitzvah, I baked 1,000 cookies – gradually over a three-month period. They looked delicious and tasted as fresh as if they were baked that same day. All it takes is a little careful planning, proper freezer wrapping (see Chapter 1), and a big freezer (or a generous friend with a big freezer).

And I do plan a particular cookie menu depending on the event, the time of year, and who will be there. So for a brunch, I tend toward the less sweet kinds of cookies and those using fruits and nuts; for weddings, I lean toward the delicate, lighter varieties often with lemon or liqueur flavorings. For children, I go for anything with chocolate morsels, shapes, and colored sugar crystals. But more about versatility in Chapter 7.

BAKING WITH KIDS, PRESENTATION, PACKAGING ARE IMPORTANT

Actually I find these subjects very important indeed, so I've devoted fuller discussion of them elsewhere in this book. You'll find:

COOKIES ARE ALWAYS IN STYLE

My publisher tells me that cookies are in vogue right now. I have to smile to myself as I try to think when, in my seventy-plus years, have cookies ever been out of style!

True, there are some new "in" kinds of cookies, but those never seem to replace the old favorites that are gobbled up as quickly as I set out a platterful.

I do test new recipes often, although I tend to fall back on my own personal favorites which I have been baking over the past 50 years. Force of habit, I guess.

But I don't claim to have originated many of these recipes. Oh, I've altered them, added a bit of this, a dash of that, often because that's what I happened to have on hand, and if it turned out tastier than the original recipe, why I changed it for the better. Recipes seem to go full circle, and oftentimes I'm given a "new" recipe only to find that it's one of my early ones with a catchy name.

So where did my collection of recipes come from . . . it came from Elaine, Jane, Debbie, Susan, Ethel, Suny, Norine, Bev, Betty, Mildred, Syl, Helen, Peg, Gen, Florence, Jewel, Jeanne, Caroline, Merlene, Joyce, Frances, the ladies from Jasper, the woman on the airplane, and the one on the bus, their friends, and friends of their friends.

And they've all been baked many times over by me.

Enjoy!

CHAPTER

1

Golde's Basic Cookie How-To

Anyone can bake cookies and have them turn out well . . . most of the time! I still have batches that aren't quite right, sometimes for a recipe I've used for years. When that happens I usually blame the oven, but truthfully I don't really know what went wrong.

But with a flexible attitude, and a creative spirit, baking cookies can be one of those simple rewarding experiences.

There's no need to make a big investment in utensils. When I first started baking, I had a wood cookstove for my oven, a bowl and wooden spoon for beating the batter, and a well-used cookie sheet (which was the secret to my success). Somehow it all worked just fine.

BASIC NEEDS

- **Three cookie sheets**

Bright, heavy-gauge aluminum cookie sheets are best because they don't absorb the heat, so cookies won't burn on the bottom. If you prefer non-stick sheets, then choose light-colored ones. Have 3 so you always have one in the oven, one cooling and one to work with.

- **Timer**
- **Measuring spoons**
- **Glass measuring cups:** for liquid ingredients
- **Graduated measuring cups:** for dry ingredients
- **Wooden spoons**
- **Set of nesting bowls:** small, medium, large
- **Rubber spatula:** so no batter is wasted
- **Metal spatula:** for removing cookies from pans
- **Wire racks:** for cooling

- **Electric mix master:** not essential; a small hand-held electric mixer works fine
- **Sifter or fine sieve**
- **8- or 9-inch-square glass or metal baking pan**
- **11″ × 7″ glass or metal baking pan**
- **9″ × 13″ baking pan or 15″ × 10″ jelly-roll pan**
- **Cookie press:** needed only for a few recipes
- **Cookie cutters:** fun to collect and kids love using them, but a glass rim works fine, too
- **Rolling pin:** use a mayonnaise jar filled with water if you don't have a rolling pin

Nice but not necessary:

- **Large mix master:** works especially well on recipes where you gradually add ingredients
- **Food processor:** If you are comfortable using your food processor, then by all means, experiment with it. You can quickly process dough with a steel blade. You'll soon learn which batters mix well (especially dough-like crusts in Chapter 2).
- **Nut chopper:** A small nut chopper is wonderful especially when adding finely chopped nut meats, but you can do this by hand with a wooden bowl and hand chopper, too.
- **Microwave:** Your microwave can be a great time-saver for preparation. Use it to melt butter and chocolate pieces, warm milk and water. (Otherwise, use a double-boiler.) The microwave is also good for warming cookies to bring back that fresh-out-of-the-oven goodness, and it works wonders for refreshing almost-stale cookies.

But what the microwave does best is defrost cookies in a big hurry. Be sure to wrap them in a paper towel before reheating or defrosting.

- **Pastry blender:** Again, if you already have one, it will be very handy for many of the bar cookies in Chapter 2, but you can easily manage without one.

FOLLOW THE RECIPE

The first few times I use a recipe, I follow the instructions very carefully, always measuring exactly and adding the called-for ingredients without substitutions or additions.

Then, if I feel it needs adjustments, I begin adding a little of this, deleting a little of that, until I get the recipe the way I want it. Oftentimes, I'll delete some sugar or add a little orange or lemon rind, but not until I've perfected the original recipe.

If you, too, enjoy experimenting, be sure to write down what you are trying, and don't trust your memory. There's nothing more frustrating than baking a delicious cookie and then being unable to duplicate it because you aren't quite sure what you added.

HEALTHFUL TRADE-OFFS

If you are trying to reduce the amount of sugar and salt in your diet, you can still enjoy homebaked cookies. You'll be surprised at how easy it is. Less sugar and salt won't affect the consistency of the cookies, and you'll find the natural fruit and nut flavorings are enhanced.

You may want to experiment with more natural flavorings by using grated orange or lemon peel when you reduce sugar in a recipe. Or try adding a dash of ground cinnamon, ground nutmeg or ground ginger, or add a splash of vanilla or almond extract. And don't forget to keep abreast of new salt and sugar substitutes on the market. These products are improving and *sometimes* work in recipes, but do follow the manufacturer's recommendations as they are not interchangeable teaspoon for teaspoon with regular granulated sugar or salt.

What about some healthy trade-offs? Here are some good ideas:

- Replace white refined sugar with maple syrup, barley malt, sorghum or unsulfured molasses in the same proportions. Replace white granulated sugar with honey according to this formula: For 1 cup sugar, use ½ cup honey and decrease the liquid by ¼ cup. If there is no liquid to decrease, then increase the flour by ¼ cup. Decrease the oven temperature by 25 degrees when baking with honey because a honey batter browns quickly.
- Replace 1 cup brown sugar with ¾ cup date sugar. Or use ½ cup honey and ¼ cup date sugar.
- Increase nutrients by replacing 1 tablespoon of sugar with 1 tablespoon of unsweetened fruit juice.
- Reduce the sugar by 2-4 tablespoons and increase the vanilla or almond extract by 1 teaspoon while also increasing the ground sweet spices (nutmeg, ginger, cinnamon, cloves, and allspice) by ½ teaspoon.
- When substituting fruit juices in baking recipes, add ¼-½ teaspoon baking soda per cup of juice.

If you are interested in using wholegrain or transitional flour instead of bleached all-purpose flour, then I highly recommend a book by nutritionist Sara Sloan, which has an excellent section on working with these flours, as well as converting existing recipes to these ingredients. There are also some good "not-too-sweet sweets" recipes. It's all in *The Brown Bag Cookbook*, available for $8.95 (add $1.00 for shipping) from Williamson Publishing in Charlotte, Vermont 05445.

WHAT ABOUT CHOCOLATE?

As every true chocolate lover knows, there's no adequate substitute for the real thing. However, if chocolate is off your diet, then try baking with carob chips when recipes call for semisweet chocolate pieces. Carob has a good taste all its own, and if you don't think of it as a chocolate substitute, you may surprise yourself and really like it.

Or you can go one step further, and substitute raisins, chopped dates, shredded coconut, chopped nuts, or chopped glazed fruits in recipes which include chocolate. In most of the bar cookie recipes in Chapter 2 you can successfully work around the chocolate without sacrificing the cookie texture. They won't be chocolate cookies, but they'll still be good cookies!

BUTTER OR MARGARINE

This is an area that comes down to personal preference, dietary restraints, and cost efficiencies. If you use a particular brand of margarine for health reasons, then by all means you can bake with it, too. Some people (my daughter Elaine included) always bake with butter and feel it makes a much richer cookie that browns to that perfect honey color. Many good cooks recommend that you use at least one-third butter for your shortening, which is certainly one way to solve the dilemma. But I, personally, don't see a significant difference in overall results, and often choose margarine for my shortening. Six of one; half dozen of the other . . . you can decide for yourself.

I do, in some recipes, specifically recommend using a solid vegetable shortening, rather than butter or margarine. In these cases, follow my recommendation, and you'll have a much lighter textured cookie.

CUTTING COSTS WITH GENERIC BRANDS

Baking ingredients tend to be expensive. All those nuts, dried fruits, chocolate pieces and coconut flakes really add up, especially when you are doing a lot of baking for a big party or holiday.

Don't hesitate to buy the generic brands instead of the well-known name brands. Remember, you will be interested in a mingling of baked flavors, so you can use different standards than you might have for table foods or fresh ingredients. You'll find the generics work equally well for peanuts, chocolate pieces, powdered sugar, honey, peanut butter and jams. For example, the generic brand strawberry preserves has many fewer whole strawberries but still plenty of berry pieces which are all you need for baking.

SIFTING

If you use pre-sifted all-purpose flour, then you don't need to sift your flour before measuring. If flour is *not* pre-sifted, then sift once before measuring. In addition, I always sift the dry ingredients (flour, leavening, spices) together before adding them to the creamed butter, sugar, eggs, flavoring mixture. This guarantees a better mingling of flavors, a dispersement of all ingredients throughout the batter or dough, and therefore, a better batch of cookies.

If you have arthritis in your hands or your hands tire easily, then try using a fine sieve instead of a sifter. Simply press (actually, stir) the dry ingredients through the sieve with a wooden spoon. Works fine!

TO GREASE OR NOT TO GREASE

I tend to grease my cookie sheets for most of my recipes, because they are much easier to remove without breakage. However, greasing does encourage cookies to spread more. So for pressed cookies and cookie-cutter cookies, where shapes are more important, I usually don't grease the baking sheets.

You may find that using a non-stick pan works best for easy removal without breakage, as well as limited spreading. If you do choose to grease your pan, I recommend using a solid vegetable shortening.

As cookies cool, they get harder to remove from the pan, especially if it is ungreased. So remove them immediately to a wire rack for cooling. If for some reason they cool before you can remove them, pop them into a warm oven for a minute or two, and they should come off without breakage.

KNOW YOUR OVEN

Oven temperatures can vary as much as 50°, so get to know how your oven works, and then adjust baking times accordingly. I always set my timer a few minutes before the shortest baking time (if recipe says 18 to 20 minutes, I check in 15 minutes).

- Use the timer on your oven or purchase a small timer at the hardware store. It is so easy to forget those cookies in the oven, once you get involved in something else. So don't trust your memory – no matter how good it is.
- Remember, with cookies, even a few minutes can make a big difference, and overbaked cookies are always a disappointment.
- Be sure to preheat your oven so it will be ready when your batter is.

- Does your oven bake evenly or do the cookies in the back get done faster than those in the front? You may need to turn the pan halfway through baking time.
- Using a glass baking pan? Reduce oven temperature by 25°.

Always bake only one sheet at a time in the middle of your oven so the heat is evenly distributed. This is really very important. I think you'll be disappointed if you try to rush by putting two sheets in at once – not a good way to save time.

GETTING STARTED

Here are some general guidelines which may seem somewhat ritualistic, but actually are good baking habits to form.

Before You Start:
- Read through the complete recipe.
- Preheat your oven.
- Assemble all of your ingredients.
- Collect all of the necessary utensils.
- Grease pan.

Making the Batter:
- Always measure ingredients accurately for best results.
- Cream shortening, eggs, sugar, and flavoring together by hand or on medium speed with electric mixer. Add any liquid or melted chocolate.
- Sift flour if not pre-sifted; measure sifted flour.
- Next, sift the flour, leavening, and spices together, and then gradually add to the creamed mixture. Mix the batter together, until well-blended, and then beat by hand or with electric mixer on medium speed.

Baking:

- Spread batter evenly for bar cookies; for dropped cookies, strive for similar size to insure even baking of all cookies.
- Rotate cookie sheets so one is in oven; one is cooling; while the third one is being prepared.
- Set timer and check cookies sooner rather than later.
- Once baked, drop cookies should immediately be removed from baking sheet to cooling rack. Bar cookies can cool in the baking pan, which also should be placed on cooling rack to prevent overbaking.

One final tip: put ingredients away as you use each one. This way you'll avoid leaving something out or putting something in twice. Many a cookie batch has been saved by following this simple rule.

STORAGE

Be sure cookies have completely cooled before storing. Bar cookies are fine left in the baking pan, cut as needed, covered with foil.

Crisp drop, rolled, or shaped cookies do best when stored in a cookie jar or other container with a loose-fitting lid.

Soft cookies also do well in a cookie jar, but be sure the lid is tight-fitting. To keep them soft, place a piece of apple in the jar. Remember that cookies baked with honey tend to absorb more moisture.

FREEZING COOKIES: BAKE WHEN *YOU* WANT TO!

Almost all cookies freeze well if they are properly wrapped. I freeze mine in reuseable plastic containers and cookie tins. I always line my tins with waxed paper, and then put additional waxed paper between every layer of cookies, with a final sheet over the top cookie layer. This adequately prevents breakage and keeps cookies from sticking together.

Here are some other cookie freezing tips:
- Cool cookies completely before freezing.
- No tins or containers? Wrap in freezer paper (not waxed paper) which is moisture proof or use a coffee tin with tight-fitting lid.
- Pack only one kind of cookie in each tin or box. Never mix varieties because their flavors intermingle.
- Use air-tight containers with a good seal. Don't use cardboard boxes as the moisture seeps in.
- Avoid freezing cookies near strong-flavored foods, such as green peppers, garlic, etc. Somehow, even with careful wrapping, the cookies tend to pick up these flavors.
- Don't crowd cookies.
- Label containers carefully with cookie name, quantity, and date.
- For long-term freezing, wrap filled tins in freezer wrap.
- The shorter the time in the freezer the better the cookies, but they will stay relatively fresh if used in 3 to 4 months. After that, they begin to lose some of their flavor.
- Freeze refrigerator cookie dough, too. Simply wrap tightly in waxed paper, and then in freezer wrap. Refrigerator cookie dough should be frozen in 12″ × 2″ logs. To defrost, thaw at room temperature until dough can be handled.
- If you are going to freeze cookies which need powdered sugar sprinkled on them, wait and do this after you defrost them. This way they look absolutely fresh. The same is true for frosting cookies – wait until you are ready to use them.

Take advantage of the fact that cookies do freeze well. They make an instant homemade dessert whenever you need something special at the last minute.

DEFROSTING

It only take 10 to 15 minutes to defrost cookies. (If you have a microwave, cookies can be defrosted in 2 to 3 minutes on low.) Once defrosted, you can heat them briefly in a slow 300°F. oven to restore crispness.

MISCELLANEOUS TIPS AND REMINDERS

- Measure ingredients very carefully. Cookie-baking is precise in measurement.
- Measure dry ingredients in graduated measuring cups, leveling off with a knife.

Leveling off a Measuring Cup

- Measure liquids in a glass measuring cup, always with cup on a flat surface at eye level.
- Chill cookie dough well and keep tightly covered until you are ready to bake.
- Is your cookie dough sticky? You may have added too much liquid. Try adding a bit of flour.
- Cookie dough too dry? You may have too much flour so add some milk or cream, 1 teaspoon at a time.
- Cookies dry? Are they overbaked or did you add too much flour?
- Keep powdered sugar in a large metal salt shaker to sprinkle readily on cookies. Cinnamon works well this way, too.
- Be sure your baking sheet is completely cooled before dropping dough on it.

Sprinkling Cookies

- Cookies baked with molasses and brown sugar tend to burn easily, so check these more frequently.
- For brightly colored cookies, roll in colored sugar crystals while still warm.
- When adding food coloring to dough, remember a little goes a long, long way – 1 or 2 drops should be sufficient.
- To measure a half cup of peanut butter or solid shortening, fill glass measuring cup with half cup of water, add solid ingredient until water reaches full cup mark. Drain and remove with rubber spatula.
- Always crack eggs over a separate bowl so a spoiled egg or egg shell won't get into other ingredients.
- Never measure ingredients directly over the mixing bowl. To avoid accidentally spilling too much into the bowl, measure first over sink or counter, then add to other ingredients in mixing bowl.
- Baking in the morning? Assemble ingredients (I even measure the dry ingredients) and utensils the night before.

And remember, too, baking cookies is an enjoyable pastime, so be easy on yourself and spread the fun around by baking with a friend or child.

CHAPTER

2

Golde's Favorite Bar Cookies

Bar or pan cookies are so easy to prepare, that you'll wonder why you ever puchased the store-bought varieties. These are perfect for any impromptu gathering; many of these recipes are simple enough to whip up in your kitchen while you chat with some unexpected guests, and then serve them informally 30 minutes later. No mess, no fuss, and a warm gesture to let people know they're welcome in your home.

Bar cookies are also great for all those times when your kids are expected to bring a group snack to Brownie meetings or Little League practice, or a class party. Younger children can learn to bake some of the simple varieties like *Special Combination Cookies* or *Jam Squares* themselves. Best of all, you can cut the cookies to any size so there will always be enough if you suddenly have a bigger group than expected. In that sense, bar cookies are wonderfully versatile.

GOLDE'S BAR COOKIE BASICS

- Do grease your pan generously with vegetable shortening; be sure to cover bottom, corners and pan sides.
- Do use the specified size baking pan or very close it it.
- If you use a glass pan, reduce the oven temperature by 25°.
- Center the baking pan on the middle oven rack.
- Test to see if done 5 minutes before estimated time using same method you use for testing cakes (insert toothpick and see if it comes out clean).
- Cool thoroughly on wire rack before slicing.
- Cover pan tightly with foil to maintain freshness, as these cookies go stale quickly in open air.

- Experiment freely with these recipes using carob, coconut, dried fruit, chopped dates, raisins, nuts, ground cinnamon, ground nutmeg, preserves, grated zucchini, grated carrots, mincemeat, liqueurs for flavorings. Bar cookies are more versatile than most, and oftentimes if an experiment doesn't quite turn out, it can be resurrected as a great dessert, with a dollop of ice cream or whipped cream on top.

AVERAGE YIELDS

If you have an 8- or 9-inch-square baking pan, you can cut the squares as large as 2″ × 2″ (4 × 4 rows), yielding 16 squares, or as small as 2″ × 1″ (4 × 8 rows) yielding 32 squares. Anything much smaller is really too small, but you can see the versatility this creates.

If you have a larger baking pan, such as a 9″ × 13″ baking pan, the bars can be as large as 2⅛″ × 1½″ (6 × 6 rows) yielding 36 bars, or as small as 1⅝″ × 1½″ (8 × 6 rows) yielding 48 bars. Of course, these are approximate so don't get out your tape measure. Simply decide how many you need, and cut accordingly.

Seafoam Chews

A wonderfully sweet confection. A family favorite for many years!

Preparation time: 40 minutes
Pans: 15″ × 10″ jelly-roll pan or 9″ × 13″ baking pan, greased
Oven: 325°F. for 30 to 35 minutes
Yield: 54 small squares

Pastry:
½   cup soft butter or margarine
½   cup granulated sugar
½   cup brown sugar, packed
2   egg yolks (reserve whites)
1   teaspoon vanilla extract
2   cups all-purpose flour
2   teaspoons baking powder
1   teaspoon baking soda
½   teaspoon salt
3   tablespoons milk
1   cup (6 oz.) semisweet chocolate pieces

Topping:
2   egg whites
1   cup brown sugar, packed
¾   cup salted peanuts, coarsely chopped

Preheat oven to 325°F.

In a large bowl, cream together butter, granulated sugar and brown sugar. Beat in egg yolks and vanilla extract. Sift flour, baking powder, baking soda and salt together. Gradually add to creamed mixture and blend together. This gets quite thick, so add up to 3 tablespoons milk. Beat well into a fluffy light dough. Gently press dough into greased baking pan. Sprinkle chocolate pieces evenly over pastry and press down lightly.

In a medium bowl, beat the two egg whites until stiff. Gradually beat in the brown sugar. Spread this mixture evenly over the pastry layer. Top with chopped peanuts.

Bake for 30 to 35 minutes. Remove pan to wire rack to cool. Cut in squares when almost cool. These squares freeze very well.

Oriental Crunch

Delicious! Makes ordinary chocolate chip cookies seem bland and plain by comparison.

Preparation time: 15 to 20 minutes
Pan: 15″ × 10″ jelly-roll pan or 9″ × 13″ baking pan, greased lightly
Oven: 375°F. for 20 minutes
Yield: 48 squares

1   **cup (2 sticks) butter, very soft**
3   **tablespoons instant coffee**
½   **teaspoon salt**
½   **teaspoon almond extract**
1   **teaspoon vanilla extract**

1   **cup granulated sugar**
2   **cups all-purpose flour**
1   **cup (6 oz.) semisweet chocolate pieces**
1   **cup almonds, broken or coarsely chopped**

Preheat oven to 375°F.

In a large bowl, cream together butter, coffee, salt, almond and vanilla extracts until smooth. Gradually add sugar, beating mixture until light and creamy. Blend in flour, then chocolate pieces and nuts. Press entire mixture lightly into a pan. (Don't press down too hard as the cookies should be crisp and light, not dense.) Bake for 20 minutes.

Cool pan on wire rack for about 5 minutes. Break cooled cookies into pieces like peanut brittle *or* while still warm, score into squares; then cool and break along the squares. Either way, these are wonderful and they freeze well, too! I promise this will be an oft' requested recipe.

Dream Cake Bars

Coconut lovers really like this old-time recipe. I always like a cup of tea with Dream Cake Bars.

Preparation time: 20 minutes
Pan: 8-inch-square pan or 11″ × 7″ baking pan, ungreased
Oven: 350°F. for 10 minutes (pastry);
        350°F. for 25 to 30 minutes (with topping)
Yield: 25 bars

Pastry:
- 1 cup all-purpose flour, sifted
- ¼ cup butter or margarine, softened
- 2 tablespoons brown sugar

Topping:
- 2 eggs
- 1 cup brown sugar, packed
- ½ teaspoon baking powder
- 3 tablespoons all-purpose flour
- 1 teaspoon vanilla extract
- 1 cup walnuts, coarsely chopped
- ¾ cup coconut, shredded

Preheat oven to 350°F.

In a medium bowl, mix pre-sifted flour, butter and 2 tablespoons brown sugar. Knead into light dough. Press gently into pan. Bake for 10 minutes.

Meanwhile, in a medium bowl, beat the two eggs lightly with a fork. Then add the remaining topping ingredients and mix thoroughly. Spread topping over partially baked pastry. Return pan to oven and bake an additional 25 to 30 minutes, until golden.

Cool completely on wire rack before cutting into squares. These freeze very well.

Light Lemon Squares

These are wonderfully light and tart. A favorite served with fresh fruit cup or sherbet.

Preparation time: 25 minutes
Pan: 8-inch-square pan, greased
Oven: 350°F. for 20 minutes (pastry);
      350°F. for 20 to 25 minutes (with topping)
Yield: 20 squares

Pastry:
1   cup all-purpose flour
½   cup (1 stick) butter or margarine
⅓   cup powdered sugar

Topping:
2   eggs
1   cup granulated sugar
½   tablespoon all-purpose flour
3   tablespoons lemon juice concentrate

Preheat oven to 350°F.

In a medium bowl, mix the pastry ingredients together. Press into a greased pan. Bake for 20 minutes.

Combine all topping ingredients together and beat until well-blended. Pour over baked pastry. Return to oven, and bake an additional 20 to 25 minutes.

Cool pan on wire rack before cutting. Sprinkle with additional sifted powdered sugar. These freeze quite well, although I think they taste fresher and lighter when freshly baked.

Chocolate Peanut Butter Fantasies

My grandchildren love these because they taste like chocolate peanut butter cups. These are so sweet, almost like a candy.

Preparation time: 35 minutes
Pan: 9″ × 13″ baking pan, ungreased

Oven: 350°F. for 12 minutes.
Yield: 36 squares

Pastry:

1½ cups all-purpose flour
⅔   cup brown sugar, firmly packed
½   teaspoon baking powder
¼   teaspoon salt
¼   teaspoon baking soda
⅔   cup butter or margarine, softened
2   egg yolks, beaten
½   teaspoon vanilla extract

Topping:

1¼ cups powdered sugar
¾   cup unsalted peanuts, finely chopped
¼   cup butter or margarine, melted
1½ cups peanut butter
½   teaspoon vanilla extract
1   (12 oz.) package semisweet chocolate pieces

Preheat oven to 350°F.

Combine all the pastry ingredients together in a large bowl, and beat at low speed until it is a crumbly consistency. Press crumbs into an ungreased baking pan. Bake for 12 minutes or until golden brown.

Set aside chocolate pieces. In medium bowl, mix remaining topping ingredients together and set aside.

Turn off the oven and remove baked pastry. Let it cool for about 2 minutes, and while still warm spread the topping evenly over the pastry. Sprinkle chocolate pieces over the topping and return to warm oven for 2 to 3 minutes until chocolate has softened enough to spread. Remove from oven and spread chocolate evenly, like a frosting. Cool before cutting.

Merlene's Hermits

These can be baked as a bar cookie or they can be formed into a drop cookie. Either way, they are rich, chewy, and spicy just like Hermits should be!

Preparation time: 20 minutes
Pan: 1 cookie sheet, greased
Oven: 325°F. for 25 minutes
Yield: 48 bars

1	cup butter or margarine, softened	3¼	cups all-purpose flour
1½	cups granulated sugar	1	teaspoon baking soda
1	teaspoon ground allspice	½	teaspoon salt
1	teaspoon ground cinnamon	½	cup molasses
1	teaspoon ground cloves	1	cup seedless raisins
3	eggs	½	cup nuts, chopped (optional)

Preheat oven to 325°F.

In large bowl, cream together the butter, sugar and spices. Add eggs, one at a time, blending them into the creamed mixture. Then add all remaining ingredients, and mix thoroughly. Spread cookie batter on greased cookie sheet. Bake for 25 minutes. Cut into bars while still warm, and cool cookies on wire rack. Makes 48 bars which freeze beautifully.

Variation: If you prefer drop cookies, preheat oven to 375°F. Drop batter by rounded teaspoonfuls onto greased cookie sheet. Bake for 12 to 15 minutes; check often so these don't burn around the edges. Cool cookies on wire rack.

Special Combination Cookies

These are so easy that the kids love making them. So delicious that everyone loves eating them.

Preparation time: 10 minutes
Pan: 9″ × 13″ baking pan, ungreased
Oven: 375°F. for 20 to 30 minutes
Yield: 48 squares

½ cup (1 stick) butter or margarine
1 cup graham cracker crumbs
1 cup flaked coconut
1 (12 oz.) package semisweet chocolate pieces
1 can sweetened condensed milk
½ cup chopped nuts (walnuts, peanuts or pecans)

Preheat oven to 375°F.

Melt butter in baking pan. Add remaining ingredients to baking pan, one at a time, in layers – i.e., first a layer of all the graham cracker crumbs, then a layer of all of the coconut, until all ingredients have been layered. Do not stir. Bake for 25 to 30 minutes. Cool pan on wire rack. Cut in squares. These are never quite as good after being frozen, but they are so quick and easy, that there really is no need to make them in advance.

Variations: Substitute 16 ounces glazed fruit for chocolate pieces, or 12 ounces of raisins, dates, and prunes (chopped).

Pecan Pie Treasures

A pecan pie lovers dream come true! These taste as good as pecan pie with much less effort. Wonderful served with whipped cream or ice cream on top.

Preparation time: 25 minutes
Pan: 9-inch-square baking pan, greased
Oven: 350°F. for 15 minutes (pastry);
       350°F. for 25 to 30 minutes (topping)
Yield: 32 bars

Pastry:
1   cup all-purpose flour
½   cup quick rolled oats, uncooked
½   cup butter or margarine, softened
¾   cup brown sugar, firmly packed

Topping:
1   tablespoon all-purpose flour
3   eggs
¾   cup dark corn syrup
¾   cup pecans, coarsely chopped
½   teaspoon vanilla extract
Dash of salt

Preheat oven to 350°F.

In medium bowl, combine all pastry ingredients. Mix together until a crumbly mixture is formed. Press into greased baking pan. Bake 15 minutes.

Meanwhile, combine the topping ingredients, mixing thoroughly. Pour over baked pastry, and bake for an additional 25 to 30 minutes, until golden brown.

Cool pan on wire rack before cutting into bars. These freeze perfectly, and are wonderful to have on hand for a quick dessert. Try topping with coffee ice cream, or whipped cream flavored with Grand Marnier.

Toffee Bars

Not-too-sweet with lots of crunch, this versatile bar cookie has special appeal when served with a steaming mug of fresh-brewed coffee.

Preparation time: 20 minutes
Pan: 9″ × 13″ baking pan, greased
Oven: 375°F. for 15 minutes
Yield: 48 small bars

Pastry:
½   cup butter or margarine, softened
½   cup light brown sugar, firmly packed
1   egg yolk
1   teaspoon vanilla extract
½   cup all-purpose flour, sifted
½   cup quick rolled oats, uncooked

Topping:
3   squares semisweet chocolate
1   tablespoon butter or margarine
½   cup walnuts or pecans, coarsely chopped

Preheat oven to 375°F.

In a large bowl, cream butter, sugar, vanilla extract, and egg yolk until smooth. Add the sifted flour and rolled oats. Stir until well-blended.

Press dough into pan. Bake 15 minutes or until golden. Remove from oven; cool slightly.

Meanwhile, melt chocolate and butter in a double boiler over hot, but not boiling water. Spread chocolate mixture over warm baked pastry. Sprinkle with nuts.

Score into bars while still warm. Cool completely before removing from pan.

Apricot Squares

*These squares are so easy to make, yet so lovely, light, and elegant.
Just right served with tea in your favorite china cups.*

Preparation time: 10 minutes
Pan: 15″ × 10″ jelly-roll pan or 9″ × 13″ baking pan, greased
Oven: 350°F. for 30 minutes
Yield: 32 squares

Pastry:
2   cups all-purpose flour
1   cup (2 sticks) butter or
    margarine, softened
2   egg yolks

1   teaspoon vanilla extract
¾   cup brown sugar, packed

Topping:
10 oz. jar apricot preserves
½   cup nuts, coarsely chopped

Preheat oven to 350°F.

In a medium bowl, combine all pastry ingredients and mix thoroughly
until light dough forms. Press into greased pan. Spread apricot preserves
evenly over pastry. Sprinkle chopped nuts on top.

Bake for 30 minutes. Remove from oven; score into squares but leave
in baking pan. Return pan to oven with heat turned off for 15 minutes
more. Complete cooling on rack.

Apricot Squares don't freeze well, as they tend to break, but they are
so easy to prepare that you'll find yourself baking them quite often.

Variations: You can substitute any kind of preserves (the thicker the
better); I often use ginger-marmalade. I usually use chopped walnuts, but
again, use what you most enjoy. If you are a coconut fan, then sprinkle
some on instead of the nuts.

Honey Zucchini-Nut Bars

Chewy, nutty, and extra moist, these are as good as they sound. A nice way to use extra large zucchinis, too.

Preparation time: 20 minutes
Pan: 9″ × 13″ baking pan, greased
Oven: 350°F. for 25 to 30 minutes
Yield: 40 bars

Pastry:
¼ cup butter, melted
1 cup honey
3 eggs, well-beaten
1¼ cups all-purpose flour
1 teaspoon baking powder
¾ cup shredded zucchini, squeezed dry

1 cup dates, finely chopped
1 cup walnuts, chopped
Dash of salt

Topping:
⅓ cup sifted powdered sugar

Preheat oven to 350°F.

Mix pastry ingredients together in order listed. Spread into greased baking pan. Bake for 25 to 30 minutes, until lightly brown. Cut into finger-sized pieces. While still warm, roll in sifted powdered sugar. These freeze well, but roll in powdered sugar *after* removing from freezer.

Variation: This recipe is good with 1 cup sunflower nutmeats instead of walnuts.

Golde's Best Brownies

I have to admit – these are so good that you'll never settle for anything less again. It's a brownie worth raving about!

Preparation time: 30 minutes
Pan: 9″ × 13″ baking pan, greased
Oven: 350°F. for 25 minutes
Yield: 60 brownies

1 cup vegetable shortening	1½ teaspoons salt
4 squares semisweet chocolate	2 teaspoons vanilla
4 eggs, beaten slightly	1 cup nuts, chopped (optional)
2 cups granulated sugar	3 tablespoons light corn syrup
1½ cups all-purpose flour	
1 teaspoon baking powder	

Preheat oven to 350°F.

In the top of a double boiler, melt the shortening and chocolate, watching carefully to avoid scorching. Pour into a large bowl. (Be sure to use a rubber spatula to get all the chocolate out of the saucepan.) Add the lightly beaten eggs, and then gradually add the sugar, mixing thoroughly.

Sift together the flour, baking powder and salt. Add to the chocolate mixture and blend well. Lastly, mix in the vanilla, nuts and syrup.

Pour batter into greased pan and bake for 25 minutes. Cool pan on wire rack. Cut into squares when cool. These freeze perfectly, and are still delicious as long as 6 months later.

Everyone's Favorite Cream Cheese Brownies

As popular as cream cheese brownies have become, this is still my old favorite recipe.

Preparation time: 30 minutes
Pan: 8- or 9-inch square, greased
Oven: 350°F. for 35 to 40 minutes
Yield: 24 brownies

Chocolate batter:

4   ounces German's sweet chocolate
3   tablespoons butter or margarine
2   eggs, beaten
¾   cup granulated sugar
½   teaspoon baking powder
¼   teaspoon salt
½   cup all-purpose flour
½   cup nuts, chopped

Preheat oven to 350°F.

1   teaspoon vanilla extract

Cheese batter:

2   tablespoons butter
1   (3 oz.) package cream cheese
¼   cup granulated sugar
1   egg
1   tablespoon all-purpose flour
½   teaspoon vanilla extract

In a double boiler, melt the chocolate with 3 tablespoons butter, stirring constantly. Set aside to cool.

Meanwhile, in medium bowl, beat 2 eggs until thick and lemon colored. Gradually add ¾ cup granulated sugar, beating until thickened. Add baking powder, salt and ½ cup flour. Once chocolate is cool, blend it in along with the nuts, and 1 teaspoon vanilla extract. Set aside.

In small bowl, cream 2 tablespoons butter with the cream cheese. Gradually add ¼ cup sugar. Cream well after each additional ingredient. Blend in 1 egg, 1 tablespoon flour, ½ teaspoon vanilla extract.

Spread about half of the chocolate batter in a greased 8- or 9-inch baking pan. Then layer on all of the cheese batter. Spoon on the remaining chocolate batter in various spots. Zigzag through the batter with a rubber spatula in order to create a marbling effect.

Bake for 35 to 40 minutes. Cool on wire rack before cutting into squares.

This freezes beautifully as long as you are sure to put waxed paper between layers.

Melting Chocolate

Double-Fudge Brownies Supreme

Prepare Golde's Best Brownies (page 39), but do not cut into squares. Frost with this topping and you'll have a wonderfully rich (but not too sweet) chocolate dessert.

Frosting preparation time: 15 minutes

2 squares semisweet chocolate	½ cup granulated sugar
1 tablespoon butter or margarine	1 tablespoon cornstarch
	¾ cup milk
	½ teaspoon vanilla extract

In a heavy saucepan, melt the butter and chocolate together being careful not to scorch the mixture. Add sugar and cornstarch and blend thoroughly. Add milk and continue cooking, stirring constantly, until thick frosting consistency. Stir in vanilla.

Cool thoroughly and spread over *Golde's Best Brownies*. Let frosted brownies set for 10 minutes before cutting into large cake-like squares.

Lemony Pecan Bars

The lemon and pecan flavors meld so well together. These will become a favorite, especially for summertime picnics and barbecues.

Preparation time: 30 minutes
Pan: 9" × 13" baking pan, greased
Oven: 325°F. for 15 minutes (pastry);
       325°F. for 35 to 40 minutes with topping
Yield: 30 bars

Pastry:
½   cup butter or margarine, softened
2   cups all-purpose flour, sifted
½   cup powdered sugar

Topping:
4   eggs, slightly beaten
1½   cups granulated sugar
½   cup lemon juice concentrate
½   teaspoon baking powder
1   cup pecans, coarsely chopped

Preheat oven to 325°F.

In a large bowl, cream together all the pastry ingredients until well-blended. Press the mixture evenly into a greased baking pan. Bake for 15 minutes.

Meanwhile, combine all topping ingredients. Stir well. Pour over the baked pastry. Return to oven and bake an additional 35 to 40 minutes or until golden brown. Cool pan on wire rack. Sprinkle with sifted powdered sugar if desired. Cut into bars when cool.

Oatmeal Date Bars

Rich with brown sugar, these are popular with oatmeal cookie lovers. They go perfectly with a glass of cold milk, too!

Preparation time: 40 minutes
Pan: 9″ × 13″ baking pan, greased
Oven: 400°F. for 20 to 25 minutes
Yield: 48 bars

Filling:
2   (8 oz.) packages dates, chopped
⅔   cup water
¾   cup granulated sugar
2   tablespoons lemon juice concentrate

Pastry:
1½   cups flour, sifted
1   cup brown sugar, packed
1½   cups quick-cooking rolled oats, uncooked
½   teaspoon salt
¾   cup vegetable shortening

Preheat oven to 400°F.

In a heavy sauce pan, combine all filling ingredients and cook about 8 minutes or until thick. Set aside to cool.

Sift flour before measuring. In a large bowl, combine flour, brown sugar, oats and salt. Cut in the shortening until coarse crumbs form.

Press half of pastry in the pan. Cover the pastry with all of the filling. Spread remaining pastry over the top.

Bake for 20 to 25 minutes until golden. Remove to wire rack. Cool before cutting into squares. These freeze very well.

Coffee-Pecan Chewies

The hint of coffee combined with pecans produces a provocative confection.

Preparation time: 35 minutes
Pan: 8-inch-square pan, greased
Oven: 350°F. for 35 minutes
Yield: 24 bars

¾	cup all-purpose flour	¼	cup butter, melted
1	teaspoon instant coffee	1	teaspoon vanilla extract
½	teaspoon salt	½	cup pecans, coarsely chopped
2	eggs	⅓	cup sifted powdered sugar
1	cup sugar		

Preheat oven to 350°F.

Sift flour, coffee and salt. Set aside.

In a large bowl, beat eggs until foamy. Add sugar and continue beating until stiff peaks form. Stir in melted butter and vanilla extract.

Add dry sifted ingredients and mix well. Fold in nuts.

Bake for 35 minutes until golden brown. Remove pan to wire rack. Cool before cutting. Sprinkle with powdered sugar if desired.

These freeze very well.

Fruit Squares

Quick and easy, yet oh-so-good. This recipe is ideal when baking with young children — just enough mixing, patting, spreading and decorating to keep them interested (and very proud when they're done).

Preparation time: 10 minutes
Pan: 9″ × 13″ baking pan, greased
Oven: 350°F. for 18 to 20 minutes
Yield: 48 squares

Pastry:
¾ cup butter or margarine
⅓ cup powdered sugar
1½ cups all-purpose flour

Topping:
10 ounce jar of favorite jam or preserve
1 cup coconut flakes (optional)
1 cup chopped nuts (optional)

Preheat oven to 350°F.

In a medium bowl, blend the pastry ingredients together. Press dough into a 9″ × 13″ greased pan. Spread your favorite preserves evenly over pastry. Sprinkle with flaked coconut or chopped nuts.

Bake for 18 to 20 minutes. For best results, refrigerate for several hours before cutting into squares.

Variation 1: I use apricot, peach, raspberry or strawberry preserves. You may want to mix two kinds together. Or you may want to bake half a panful in one flavor, the other half pan in another flavor for both color and flavor contrasts.

Variation 2: For added flavor and a bit of tang to offset the sweetness, grate about 1 tablespoon orange or lemon peel into the preserves before spreading.

Variation 3: If you prefer sprinkling with chopped nuts instead of coconut before baking, try using sunflower nutmeats. Shake some powdered sugar on when you remove the pan from the oven, while squares are still hot.

Grating citrus peels

Applesauce n'Fudge Bars

The applesauce keeps these moist and fresh. The chocolate gives them a fudgy richness.

Preparation time: 20 minutes
Pan: 8- or 9-inch-square pan, greased
Oven: 350°F. for 30 minutes
Yield: 24 bars

2	squares unsweetened chocolate	1	teaspoon vanilla extract
½	cup (1 stick) butter or margarine	1	cup all-purpose flour, sifted
⅔	cup sweetened applesauce	½	teaspoon baking powder
2	eggs, beaten	¼	teaspoon baking soda
1	cup brown sugar, firmly packed	¼	teaspoon salt
		½	cup walnuts, chopped

Preheat oven to 350°F.

Melt chocolate and butter together. Set aside.

In a large bowl, mix applesauce, eggs, sugar, and vanilla extract together. Sift the dry ingredients together. Gradually mix into the applesauce mixture. Blend well. Add melted chocolate and stir well.

Pour into greased pan. Sprinkle with chopped walnuts. Bake for 30 minutes. Remove pan to rack and cool. Cut into bars.

These freeze well, and stay fresh (if well-covered) for an unusually long time.

Chocolate Chip Cookie Bars

A favorite with kids of all ages and so easy to make.

Preparation time: 20 to 25 minutes
Pan: 15″ × 10″ jelly-roll pan, ungreased
Oven: 350°F. for 20 minutes
Yield: 48 bars

1	cup butter or margarine, very soft	Dash salt	
1	cup light brown sugar, packed	1	cup 6 oz.) semisweet chocolate pieces
1	teaspoon vanilla extract	¾	cup pecans or walnuts, coarsely chopped
2	cups flour		

Preheat oven to 350°F.

In a large bowl, beat the butter and sugar until fluffy. Add the vanilla extract. Sift the salt plus flour into the butter mixture and blend well. Fold in chocolate pieces and nuts.

Press batter into an ungreased jelly-roll pan. Bake for 20 minutes until golden brown. While warm score into bars and cool in pan on wire rack.

Freeze very well if they last that long!

Heavenly Chocolate Nut Meltaways

Ahhh . . . and what a heavenly treat these are! A surprise chocolate layer wrapped in a light pastry with a rich, nutty topping.

Preparation time: 40 minutes
Pan: 9″ × 13″ baking pan, greased
Oven: 350°F. for 10 minutes (pastry);
       350°F. for 30 to 35 minutes (topping)
Yield: 48 squares

Pastry:
½ cup (1 stick) butter or margarine
1 egg yolk
2 tablespoons water
1½ cups all-purpose flour
1 teaspoon granulated sugar
1 teaspoon baking powder
1 cup (6 oz.) semisweet chocolate pieces

Preheat oven to 350°F.

Topping:
2 eggs
¾ cups granulated sugar
6 tablespoons butter or margarine, melted
2 teaspoons vanilla extract
2 cups nuts, coarsely chopped

To make pastry, in a medium bowl, beat together the ½ cup butter, egg yolk, and water. Stir in the flour, 1 teaspoon sugar and baking powder. Mix together. Pat into a greased 9″ × 13″ pan. Bake for 10 minutes.

Remove from oven, and sprinkle with chocolate pieces. Return to oven for 1 minute to melt. Remove from oven and spread chocolate as you would a frosting. Set aside.

To make the topping, in a small bowl, beat the 2 eggs and ¾ cup sugar together. Stir in the melted butter and vanilla extract. When well-blended, fold in the chopped nuts. Spread topping over chocolate layer. Bake in 350° oven for 30 to 35 minutes. Remove to wire rack to cool. Cut into squares while still warm, but leave in pan until ready to use or freeze.

Spreading the Chocolate Pieces

Creamy Cheesecake Bars

As rich and creamy as the best cheesecake, and much easier to bake. This recipe is a longtime staple of mine, still the best one of its kind.

Preparation time: 25 minutes
Pan: 8-inch-square pan, ungreased
Oven: 350°F. for 12 to 15 minutes (pastry);
        350°F. for 25 to 30 minutes (filling)
Yield: 36 bars

Pastry:
⅓ cup butter or margarine, softened
⅓ cup brown sugar, firmly packed
1   cup all-purpose flour, sifted
⅓ cup walnuts, finely chopped

Filling:
¼ cup granulated sugar
1   (8 oz.) package cream cheese, softened
1   egg, beaten
2   tablespoons milk
1   tablespoon lemon juice
½ teaspoon vanilla extract

Preheat oven to 350°F.

In a medium bowl, cream the butter and brown sugar together until light. Add the sifted flour and chopped walnuts. Mix until crumbs form. Set aside 2 cups to use as topping. Press remaining crumb mixture into ungreased pan. Bake for 12 to 15 minutes. Cool pan on rack.

Meanwhile, in a small bowl, beat the granulated sugar and cream cheese until smooth. Add remaining ingredients and beat thoroughly.

Spread this mixture over the baked crumb crust. Sprinkle reserved crumbs as a topping.

Bake for 25 to 30 minutes. Remove pan to rack to cool. Cut in bars and refrigerate as these will spoil if left unrefrigerated. Garnish each square with a half of a strawberry if you like. These freeze very well.

Date-Nut Squares

If you like the chewiness of dates, you'll love these. A perfect cookie for brunch or tea on a brisk autumn day.

Preparation time: 30 minutes
Pan: 9" × 13" baking pan, greased
Oven: 350°F. for 20 to 25 minutes
Yield: 60 small squares

¾ cup all-purpose flour	1 cup granulated sugar
¼ teaspoon baking powder	2 eggs, beaten
⅛ teaspoon salt (optional)	1 cup walnuts, chopped fine
½ cup butter or margarine, melted	1 cup dates, cut fine
	½ cup powdered sugar

Preheat oven to 350°F.

Sift flour, baking powder and salt together; set aside.

In a medium bowl, mix together melted butter, sugar and beaten eggs. When well-blended, gradually add sifted dry ingredients. Mix well and fold in nuts and dates.

Spread dough on greased baking pan, and bake for 20 to 25 minutes. Remove pan to wire rack and cut in bars while still warm. Roll warm squares in powdered sugar.

To freeze: Freeze squares before rolling in powdered sugar. After defrosting, warm squares in 300°F. oven for 3 to 5 minutes, and then proceed to roll in powdered sugar. Cookies will look much fresher this way!

Butter Pecan Turtle Bars

The brown sugar gives these a rich color, and a very rich flavor.

Preparation time: 35 to 40 minutes
Pan: 9″ × 13″ baking pan, ungreased
Oven: 350°F. for 18 to 20 minutes
Yield: 42 bars

Pastry:
2   cups all-purpose flour
1   cup brown sugar, firmly packed
½   cup sweet butter, softened
1-1½ cups pecan halves

Topping:
⅔   cup sweet butter
½   cup brown sugar, firmly packed
1   cup (6 oz.) semisweet chocolate pieces

Preheat oven to 350°F.

In a medium bowl, blend flour, 1 cup brown sugar and ½ cup softened sweet butter on medium speed (or by hand with a fork) until mixture is in fine particles. Press firmly into ungreased 9″ × 13″ baking pan. Sprinkle pecans evenly over unbaked pastry.

In heavy saucepan, combine ⅔ cup sweet butter and ½ cup brown sugar. Cook over medium heat, stirring constantly, until entire surface begins to boil. Continue boiling for 1 minute while still stirring. Pour mixture over the pastry.

Bake for 18 to 20 minutes or until topping layer is bubbly and pastry is golden brown.

Remove pan from oven to wire rack and sprinkle with chocolate pieces. Do not spread. Allow chocolate pieces to melt slightly and then swirl as they melt. Leave some chocolate pieces whole.

Cool and cut into bars. These freeze well. A wonderful treat!

Spicy Applesauce-Raisin Squares

Bake these in the fall when you're making homemade applesauce. They'll fill your kitchen with a spicy aroma, and you'll know that autumn is here.

Preparation time: 35 minutes
Pan: 15" × 10" jelly-roll pan or 9" × 13" baking pan, greased
Oven: 350°F. for 25 minutes
Yield: 36 squares

2 cups all-purpose flour, sifted	1 egg
2 teaspoons baking soda	1 teaspoon vanilla extract
¾ teaspoon ground cinnamon	1½ cups applesauce
¼ teaspoon ground cloves	¾ cup walnuts or pecans, chopped
¼ teaspoon ground nutmeg	¾ cup light or dark seedless raisins
½ cup (1 stick) butter or margarine, softened	Powdered sugar
1 cup granulated sugar	

Preheat oven to 350°F.

Sift pre-sifted flour, baking soda, and three spices together. Set aside.

In a large bowl, cream butter and sugar together until fluffy. Add the egg and vanilla extract and beat well. Add the sifted flour mixture, and mix just enough to combine. Add applesauce, nuts and raisins. Stir with spoon until well-blended.

Bake for 20 to 25 minutes. Remove pan to wire rack to cool.

Sprinkle with sifted powdered sugar, and cut into squares. Or, these can be cut into large cake-like squares and served with a dollop of homemade whipped cream.

Lemony Coconut Delights

These two flavors belong together. Here they're made even richer by the brown sugar filling.

Preparation time: 35 minutes
Pan: 9″ × 13″ baking pan, greased
Oven: 325°F. for 10 to 15 minutes (pastry);
      350°F. for 20 minutes (filling)
Yield: 48 squares

Pastry:
1½   cups all-purpose flour, sifted
½   cup brown sugar, firmly packed
½   cup butter or margarine, softened

Topping:
1   cup powdered sugar
1   tablespoon butter or margarine, melted
Juice of 1 lemon
½   teaspoon grated lemon rind

Filling:
2   eggs, beaten
1   cup brown sugar, firmly packed
1   cup flaked coconut
1   cup nuts, chopped
2   tablespoons all-purpose flour
½   teaspoon baking powder
¼   teaspoon salt
¼   teaspoon vanilla extract

Preheat oven to 325°F.

In a medium bowl, mix together pastry ingredients until a dough forms. Press the dough into a greased baking pan. Bake for 10 to 15 minutes. Remove from oven. Reset oven to 350°.

In the meantime, combine all the filling ingredients in a small bowl. Mix until well-blended. Spread over pastry and bake for 20 minutes at 350°F.

Mix topping ingredients together. While cookies are still warm, spread topping over baked pastry. Cool slightly and cut into squares.

CHAPTER

3

Golde's Best Drop Cookies

Drop cookies demand a bit more time and attention, but they are still easy to prepare and are well worth any extra effort. There is nothing quite like the look of a smiling face crunching into a *Chocolate Chip Crisper* or a cinnamon *Snickerdoodle*. And drop cookies, after all, are what we think of when we think of "cookies," or cookie jar, or even Cookie Monster!

Here are a few do's and don'ts to help you have success with every batch you bake.

- Spoon by the rounded or heaping (for larger cookies) teaspoonful, using a regular flatware teaspoon rather than a measuring teaspoon. Use a rubber spatula to push batter onto cookie sheet.
- Strive for general uniformity in size and shape; this way all your cookies will be done at approximately the same time.
- Leave adequate space between teaspoonfuls of cookie batter; remember these cookies spread as they bake. I usually leave about 2 inches between medium-sized cookies.
- Be sure to grease cookie sheets adequately, unless otherwise directed. I recommend using vegetable shortening for this. If your cookies spread too much, then cut down on greasing or use a non-stick pan. If you don't use grease, be sure to remove cookies from the sheet while still hot.
- Keep close watch on cookies while they bake until you really get to know your oven and your cookie sheet. Drop cookies bake very quickly and are apt to burn around the edges or on the bottom if not closely tended.
- Remove cookies from the cookie sheets as soon as possible to stop the baking process. Cool cookies on wire racks (raised slightly above counter) for best results.

- Drop cookies are perfect for double-batching. Consider always doubling your recipe – some for now and some all baked and popped into the freezer.
- Giant-sized cookies are popular now. Just use more batter and, of course, adjust space between each to allow for spreading. Kids love these, plus they're great fun at picnics. Try *Chocolate Chip Crispers, Crispy Oatmeal-Raisin Cookies, and Spicy Fruit Cookies* (all in Chapter 3) for giants.
- Drop cookies aren't as versatile as bar cookies when it comes to altering recipes. You can feel fairly confident about interchanging kinds of nuts, sunflower seed meats, raisins, chopped dates, chopped apricots, carob bits, chocolate pieces, butterscotch pieces, flavored extracts, and flaked coconut, but keep the basic batter as recommended in each recipe.

Putting Batter onto Cookie Sheet

Chocolate Meringue Fluffs

Chocolate fanciers will love these chocolaty, chewy meringues. Be sure to double your batch because these go as fast as you can refill the platter!

Preparation time: 30 minutes
Pan: cookie sheets, greased
Oven: 350°F. for 10 minutes
Yield: 80 cookies

1 cup (6 oz.) semisweet chocolate pieces	⅓ cup graham cracker crumbs
3 egg whites	½ teaspoon vanilla extract
1 cup granulated sugar	

Preheat oven to 350°F.

In a double boiler or microwave, melt the chocolate pieces. Let chocolate cool for 5 minutes.

Meanwhile, in a medium bowl beat egg whites until stiff, but not too dry. Gradually add the sugar and beat until smooth and glossy. Fold in, with a wooden spoon, the melted chocolate, the graham cracker crumbs and the vanilla extract.

Drop by level teaspoonfuls onto greased cookie sheet. Bake for 10 minutes. Cool cookies on baking sheet for 2 to 3 minutes for easier removal.

Chocolate Meringue Fluffs freeze fairly well, though they tend to lose some of their fluffy texture once frozen, and they break easily. So I'd suggest you freeze some other kind, and save these quick and easy meringues for immediate use.

Chocolate Chip Crispers

Sweet and chewy! Kids eat these as fast as I can bake them.

Preparation time: 30 minutes
Pan: cookie sheets, greased
Oven: 350°F. for 12 minutes
Yield: 52 cookies

½	cup butter or margarine, softened	1¼	cups all-purpose flour
1	cup granulated sugar	½	teaspoon baking soda
1	egg	¼	teaspoon salt
1	teaspoon vanilla extract	2	cups Rice Crispies®
		1	cup (6 oz.) semisweet chocolate pieces

Preheat oven to 350°F.

In a large bowl, beat butter and sugar until smooth. Beat in the egg and vanilla extract. Set aside.

In a small bowl, combine flour, baking soda, and salt and mix together well.

Add flour mixture to the batter and mix until well-blended. Stir in the Rice Crispies® and chocolate pieces.

Drop by level tablespoonfuls onto greased cookie sheet. Bake about 12 minutes or until light brown. Remove cookies to wire rack to cool.

These freeze well if you can keep them around that long.

Walnut Surprise

A chewy, nutty cookie that is simply delicious. My favorite for serving with fresh fruit mélange for dessert.

Preparation time: 30 minutes
Pan: cookie sheet, ungreased
Oven: 350°F. for 10 to 12 minutes
Yield: 30 cookies

Pastry:
½   cup butter or margarine, softened
1   cup dark brown sugar, packed
1   egg, well-beaten
½   teaspoon vanilla extract
2¼ cups all-purpose flour

1   teaspoon baking soda
Dash salt

Filling:
¾   cups walnuts, finely chopped
½   cup plus 1 tablespoon brown sugar
¼   cup sour cream

Preheat oven to 350°F.

In a large bowl, cream together the butter and brown sugar. Add the egg and vanilla. Beat well. Sift in the flour, baking soda and salt. Mix until well-blended.

In a small bowl, mix filling ingredients together and set aside.

Drop pastry by teaspoonfuls onto ungreased cookie sheet. Make a well in each cookie with your thumb and add a scant teaspoon of filling to each.

The cookies will flatten as they bake. Bake for 10 to 12 minutes or until they are lightly browned. Cool cookies on wire racks.

These freeze perfectly and are so versatile and popular that I always make a double batch.

Variation: You can substitute pecans for the walnuts. They taste wonderful, but are more expensive.

Spicy Fruit Cookies

A wonderful cookie to bake on an early winter's day. These cookies fill the kitchen with an enticing aroma that beckons all to gather round the kitchen table for cookies and hot cider.

Preparation time: 30 minutes
Pan: cookie sheet, greased
Oven: 375°F. for 10 to 12 minutes
Yield: 70 cookies

1 cup vegetable shortening, softened	3 cups all-purpose flour
1 cup brown sugar, packed	2 teaspoons ground cinnamon
1 egg	1 teaspoon ground cloves
½ cup soured milk (½ cup milk mixed with 1 teaspoon vinegar)	1 teaspoon baking powder
½ cup molasses	1 cup raisins or 1 cup mixture raisins, chopped dates, and chopped prunes
1 teaspoon baking soda (dissolved in the milk)	

Preheat oven to 375°F.

In a large bowl, cream the vegetable shortening. Then add the sugar and egg. Blend well. Add the soured milk and molasses.

Sift the flour with the cinnamon, cloves, and baking powder. Gradually add to the molasses-butter mixture. Stir in raisins or mixed fruit.

Drop by teaspoonfuls on greased cookie sheet. Bake for 10 to 12 minutes until deep brown.

Cool cookies on wire rack. These freeze very well.

Crispy Oatmeal Raisin Cookies

Here's a less chewy oatmeal cookie, bursting with raisins and nuts.

Preparation time: 35 minutes
Pan: cookie sheets, greased
Oven: 400°F. for 10 minutes
Yield: 36 cookies

1½	cups rolled oats, uncooked	¼	teaspoon salt
½	cup granulated sugar	5	teaspoons milk or water
½	cup butter or margarine, melted	1½	teaspoons vanilla extract
1	egg, beaten	¾	cup seedless raisins
¾	cup all-purpose flour	¼	cup nuts, chopped (optional)
2	teaspoons baking powder		

Preheat oven to 400°F.

In a large bowl, combine the rolled oats and sugar. Add the melted butter and egg. Mix until well-blended. Set aside.

Sift the flour, baking powder and salt together. Add to the oat mixture, and mix well.

Add the milk, vanilla, raisins, and nuts.

Drop by rounded teaspoonfuls on greased cookie sheet. Press down each spoonful with the back of a wet spoon or fork to about ⅛ inch thickness.

Bake for 10 minutes until lightly browned. Remove to wire rack to cool. These freeze very well.

Famous Oatmeal Cookies

If you've never tested the recipe on the Quaker Oats® box, here it is – a very fine oatmeal cookie indeed!

Preparation time: 30 minutes
Pan: cookie sheet, greased
Oven: 350°F. for 12 to 15 minutes
Yield: 60 large cookies

¾	cup vegetable shortening	1	teaspoon vanilla extract
1	cup brown sugar, firmly packed	3	cups rolled oats, uncooked
½	cup granulated sugar	1	cup all-purpose flour
1	egg	½	teaspoon baking soda
¼	cup water	½	teaspoon salt (optional)

Preheat oven to 350°F.

In a large bowl, beat together shortening, brown sugar, granulated sugar, egg, water and vanilla extract until creamy. Combine remaining ingredients and add to creamed shortening mixture. Beat well.

Drop by heaping teaspoonfuls (for large cookies) onto greased cookie sheet.

Bake for 12 to 15 minutes or until golden brown. Cool cookies on wire rack. These freeze very well – I always make a double batch!

Variations: Add ½ cup chopped nuts, raisins, semisweet chocolate pieces or coconut.

Zucchini Oatmeal Drops

These are crammed with good-for-you ingredients. They make a good breakfast cookie, as well as a nice mid-morning snack.

Preparation time: 30 minutes
Pan: cookie sheet, greased
Oven: 350°F. for 12 minutes
Yield: 50 cookies

½   cup vegetable shortening
1   egg, beaten
⅛   teaspoon baking soda
¾   cup honey
1   cup all-purpose flour
1   teaspoon baking powder
Dash salt

1   cup rolled oats, uncooked
½   cup grated zucchini, drained and squeezed dry*
½   cup nuts, finely chopped
½   cup seedless raisins
1   teaspoon vanilla extract

Preheat oven to 350°F.

In a large bowl, cream together the vegetable shortening and egg. Stir the baking soda into the honey, and then add to the creamed ingredients.

Sift the flour, baking powder, and salt together into the creamed mixture.

Combine rolled oats, zucchini, nuts and raisins and stir into batter. Add vanilla extract and blend well.

Drop by rounded teaspoonfuls on greased cookie sheet. Flatten each ball by pressing with a fork. Bake for 12 minutes or until brown. Cool cookies on wire rack.

Variation: Substitute ½ cup grated carrot for the zucchini.

*Note: When zucchini seems to be growing *everywhere*, grate them in your food processor. Squeeze out water. Freeze in 1 cup and ½ cup amounts. Drain and squeeze dry again after defrosting.

Chocolate Chip-Peanut Butter Cookies

This cookie bursts with wonderful flavor. Grind your own peanut butter* for a richer peanutty taste.

Preparation time: 35 minutes
Pan: cookie sheet, ungreased
Oven: 375°F. for 8 to 10 minutes
Yield: 50 cookies

½ cup butter or margarine, softened	1 cup plus 2 tablespoons all-purpose flour
¼ cup granulated sugar	½ teaspoon salt
½ cup brown sugar, firmly packed	½ teaspoon vanilla extract
½ teaspoon baking soda	1 cup smooth or crunchy peanut butter
1 egg, beaten	1 cup (6 oz.) of semisweet chocolate pieces

Preheat oven to 375°F.

In a large bowl, cream together butter, sugar, and brown sugar. Add the remaining ingredients in the order shown, and mix until well-blended.

Drop by rounded teaspoonfuls onto an ungreased cookie sheet. Bake for 8 to 10 minutes or until golden brown. Remove to wire racks to cool.

*2 cups peanuts to 1 tablespoon peanut oil. Blend in your food processor on high until smooth or crunchy, whichever you prefer.

Original Toll House® Cookies

Some recipes simply cannot be improved upon . . . here is the all-time favorite chocolate chip cookie.

Preparation time: 20 minutes
Pan: cookie sheet, ungreased
Oven: 375°F. for 8 to 10 minutes
Yield: 100 cookies

1 cup butter or margarine, softened	1 teaspoon baking soda
¾ cup granulated sugar	1 teaspoon salt
¾ cup brown sugar, firmly packed	2 cups (12 oz.) semisweet chocolate pieces
2 eggs	1 cup chopped nuts (optional)
2¼ cups all-purpose flour	

Preheat oven to 375°F.

In a large bowl beat butter, sugar, brown sugar and eggs together until a fluffy batter forms. Set aside.

Sift together flour, baking soda and salt. Add to batter, beating until well-blended. Mix in the chocolate pieces and nuts.

Drop by rounded teaspoonfuls on ungreased cookie sheets.

Bake for 8 to 10 minutes or until lightly browned. Cool cookies on wire racks.

Chocolate Chip Meringue Kisses

These puffs of sweetness are wonderful holiday cookies. You can set them out on a silver dish like candy or pass them around at dessert time with coffee and tea.

Preparation time: 10 minutes
Pan: cookie sheet
Oven: 300°F. for 25 minutes
Yield: 36 cookies

2	egg whites (room temperature)	¾	teaspoon vanilla extract
⅛	teaspoon salt	¾	cup granulated sugar
⅛	teaspoon cream of tartar	1	cup (6 oz.) semisweet chocolate pieces

Preheat oven to 300°F. Line cookie sheet with a brown paper bag.

In a medium bowl, beat egg whites, salt, cream of tartar and vanilla extract together until smooth.

Gradually add the sugar and continue beating until batter forms peaks. Fold in the chocolate pieces.

Drop by teaspoonfuls onto lined cookie sheet. Swirl the top to look like a big chocolate kiss.

Bake for 25 minutes. Cool on wire rack. If you plan to freeze these, be sure not to crowd, as they break quite easily.

Cocoa-Pecan Drops

These are very rich, but not too sweet. The cream cheese filling brings out the best in the pecans.

Preparation time: 45 minutes
Pan: cookie sheets, ungreased
Oven: 350°F. for 10 to 12 minutes
Yield: 50 cookies

Dough:
1   cup butter, softened
1   cup powdered sugar
2   tablespoons unsweetened cocoa
1¾ cups all-purpose flour, sifted
1   egg yolk (reserve white)

Garnish:
2   egg whites
1½ cups pecans, chopped
50 pecan halves
    Preheat oven to 350°F.

Filling:
1   cup powdered sugar
1   egg yolk (reserve white)
3   tablespoons unsweetened cocoa
6   ounces (2 small packages) cream cheese, softened
1¼ teaspoons vanilla extract

In a large bowl, cream the butter and add remaining dough ingredients. Mix until very well-blended. Set aside.

In a small bowl, combine 1 cup powdered sugar and cream cheese. Cream and add remaining filling ingredients. Mix until smooth. Set aside.

Beat 2 egg whites until foamy. Set aside.

Roll dough into 50 walnut-sized balls. Dip each ball into the egg whites and then roll in chopped pecans. Place about 1 inch apart on cookie sheet. Press thumb into center of each ball, making a well. Drop 1 teaspoon of filling in each well. Adorn with pecan half.

Bake for 10 to 12 minutes. Cool on sheets for 3 minutes and remove to wire rack to complete cooling. Store in refrigerator.

Shaping Cocoa-Pecan Drops

Chocolate Thinsees

These are a small, lightly flavored tea cookie. But watch out – they can be very habit-forming.

Preparation time: 30 minutes
Pan: cookie sheet, greased
Oven: 300°F. for 10 to 12 minutes
Yield: 70 small cookies

2 squares semisweet chocolate, melted	Dash of salt
½ cup butter, softened	½ cup all-purpose flour
1 cup brown sugar, packed	¼ teaspoon vanilla extract
2 eggs	¾ cup nuts, finely chopped

Preheat oven to 300°F.

Melt chocolate in a double boiler or microwave.

Pour melted chocolate and all other ingredients (except nuts) into a medium bowl, and mix until well-blended

Drop by scant teaspoonfuls on greased cookie sheet. Sprinkle with chopped nuts.

Bake for 10 to 12 minutes. Cool pan for about 2 minutes before removing cookies to a wire rack. These cookies are sometimes difficult to remove without breaking, so be sure to wait 2 minutes and use a wide spatula.

I prefer not to freeze these, as they seem to lose something in both flavor and appearance.

Honey-Raisin Meltaways

A subtle melding of honey, brown sugar and almond flavors afloat in a light fluffy batter.

Preparation time: 25 minutes
Pan: cookie sheet, greased
Oven: 375°F. for 10 to 12 minutes
Yield: 36 cookies

¼	cup butter or margarine, softened	1	cup all-purpose flour, pre-sifted
⅓	cup brown sugar, packed	1	teaspoon baking powder
⅓	cup honey	1	teaspoon almond extract
2	eggs, separated	3	tablespoons milk
		1	cup seedless raisins

Preheat oven to 375°F.

In a large bowl, cream the butter and sugar together. Add the honey and egg yolks. Mix until well-blended. Set aside egg whites, and mix in all remaining ingredients.

Beat egg whites until they form stiff peaks. Gently fold into batter with a wooden spoon.

Drop by teaspoonfuls onto greased cookie sheets. Bake for 10 to 12 minutes. Remove to wire racks to cool. These freeze very well.

Sugar Cookies

I baked these on a wood cookstove when we lived in Jasper, New York, 40 years ago. This is still the best sugar cookie recipe I've found.

Preparation time: 25 minutes
Pan: cookie sheets, greased
Oven: 350°F. for 12 to 15 minutes
Yield: 120 cookies

1 cup vegetable shortening	1¼ cups soured milk (mix 1 cup milk with 2 tablespoons vinegar)
2 cups granulated sugar	
2 eggs	1 teaspoon vanilla extract or lemon juice concentrate
3 cups all-purpose flour	
1 teaspoon baking powder	Raisins, chopped dates, chopped walnuts, or shredded coconut (optional)
1 teaspoon baking soda	

Preheat oven to 350°F.

In a large bowl, cream the shortening. Add the sugar and eggs, and blend in thoroughly. Set aside.

Sift the flour and the baking powder into a medium bowl. Set aside. Mix the baking soda with the soured milk.

To the shortening mixture, alternately stir in the flour mixture and the milk mixture. Add the vanilla extract and any optional ingredients you wish. Mix all thoroughly.

Drop by heaping teaspoonfuls onto greased cookie sheet. Bake for 12 to 15 minutes. Sprinkle with some granulated sugar or colored sugar crystals while still warm. Remove to wire rack to cool. These freeze very well.

Coffee Cookies

A mild coffee flavor in a cookie that is not too sweet.

Preparation time: 30 minutes
Pan: cookie sheet, greased
Oven: 350°F. for 10 to 12 minutes
Yield: 30 cookies

½	cup vegetable shortening	¾	cup all-purpose flour
⅔	cup granulated sugar	½	teaspoon vanilla extract
2	tablespoons instant coffee	½	cup nuts, chopped
1	egg		(optional)

Preheat oven to 350°F.

In a medium bowl, cream together the shortening, sugar and instant coffee. Add the remaining ingredients and mix until well-blended.

Drop by rounded teaspoonfuls on greased cookie sheet. Bake for 10 to 12 minutes. Remove cookies immediately from pan and cool on a wire rack.

Variation 1: *Mocha Cookies.* Add 3 tablespoons of powdered cocoa to the batter for a rich mocha flavor.

Variation 2: *Coffee-Amaretto Cookies.* Substitute ½ teaspoon almond extract for the vanilla extract and add ½ cup toasted slivered almonds. Or add 1 teaspoon amaretto liqueur and ½ cup toasted slivered almonds. Omit the vanilla extract.

Cream Cheese Kisses

Take a rich cream cheese batter; add the tartness of lemon, the subtlety of pecans and you have a wonderfully balanced, very fine cookie.

Preparation time: 20 minutes
Pan: cookie sheets, ungreased
Oven: 300°F for 20 minutes
Yield: 60 cookies

¾ cup butter or margarine, softened
1 (3 oz.) package cream cheese, softened
1 cup powdered sugar
1 tablespoon lemon juice
2 teaspoons grated lemon peel
1 teaspoon vanilla extract
2 cups all-purpose flour
1 cup pecans, finely chopped
Powdered sugar, sifted

Preheat oven to 300°F.

In a large bowl, beat the butter and cream cheese until light and fluffy. Gradually add 1 cup powdered sugar and beat at high speed for 1 minute.

Reduce speed and mix in lemon juice, lemon peel and vanilla extract. Add the flour, and mix well. Stir in the chopped nuts.

Drop by teaspoonfuls onto ungreased cookie sheet. Bake 20 minutes, until lightly browned.

While still hot, either roll in or sprinkle with powdered sugar.

Cool on wire racks.

Peanut Butter Surprises

Here's a treat and then some . . . peanut butter plus crunchy peanuts plus chocolate pieces, all in a brown sugar cookie. These cookies get eaten so fast that you'd better always bake a double batch.

Preparation time: 30 minutes
Pan: cookie sheets, ungreased
Oven: 350°F. for 8 to 10 minutes
Yield: 100 cookies

2 cups all-purpose flour	2 eggs
2 teaspoons baking soda	1¼ teaspoons vanilla extract
½ teaspoon salt	1 cup peanut butter*
1 cup butter or margarine, softened	¾ cup peanuts, unsalted
1 cup granulated sugar	1 cup (6 oz.) package semisweet chocolate pieces
1¼ cups light brown sugar, firmly packed	

Preheat oven to 350°F.

Into a medium bowl, sift together flour, soda and salt. Set aside.

In a large bowl, cream the butter and both sugars until light. Add the eggs and vanilla extract; beat until light and fluffy.

Blend in the peanut butter. Gradually add the flour mixture. Stir in the peanuts and chocolate pieces.

Drop by teaspoonfuls onto ungreased cookie sheets. Bake for 8 to 10 minutes or until lightly browned.

Remove cookies to wire racks to cool.

Variations: Substitute butterscotch pieces for chocolate pieces or add raisins to the batter.

Helen's Christmas Cookies

Helen is ninety years old and she still bakes these for her family every Christmas. They will rival fruit cake in popularity, and will be year 'round favorites.

Preparation time: 30 minutes
Pan: cookie sheets, greased
Oven: 300°F. for 30 minutes
Yield: 72 cookies

3 cups all-purpose flour	1 small (6 oz.) jar maraschino cherries, chopped (reserve liquid)
1 teaspoon baking soda	
½ teaspoon salt	
1 cup vegetable shortening	1 (8 oz.) package dates, coarsely chopped
1½ cups granulated sugar	
3 eggs	½ cup walnuts, coarsely chopped

Preheat oven to 300°F.

In a large bowl, sift together flour, baking soda, and salt. Set aside.

In a small bowl, mix the cherries, dates and walnuts together. Pour the cherry juice over the mixture. Set aside.

Cream together the shortening and sugar. Add the eggs and blend well. Add the cherry-date mixture and mix until well-blended.

Add the creamed-cherry batter to the flour mixture and blend well.

Drop by rounded teaspoonfuls on greased cookie sheet. Bake for 30 minutes. Remove cookies to wire rack to cool.

These freeze very well.

Chocolate Macaroons

A chewy coconut treat. In the summer, these are good cold from the refrigerator, or partially frozen.

Preparation time: 25 minutes
Pan: cookie sheets, greased
Oven: 325°F. for 20 minutes
Yield: 35 macaroons

3 egg whites	1½ cups semisweet chocolate pieces, melted
¾ cup granulated sugar, sifted	2¼ cups shredded coconut
⅜ teaspoon salt	½ cup finely chopped walnuts or pecans (optional)
1 teaspoon vanilla extract	

Preheat oven to 325°F.

In a large bowl, beat egg whites until foamy. Add salt and beat a little more.

Gradually add sugar, a tablespoon at a time, beating constantly until mixture stands in peaks. Add vanilla. Fold in cooled melted chocolate. Add coconut and nuts.

Mix gently. Drop in small mounds by teaspoonfuls on a greased cookie sheet.

Bake for 15 to 20 minutes. Do not overbake. Cookies must still be slightly soft in center. Remove pan to wire rack. Cool a few minutes and then use a spatula to loosen cookies from pan.

These freeze very well.

Lacey Wafers

Mildly flavored, these delicate cookies are perfect when served with fresh fruit and dessert cheeses.

Preparation time: 20 minutes
Pan: cookie sheets, lined with foil
Oven: 325°F. for 8 to 10 minutes
Yield: 24 cookies

¼   cup light corn syrup
¼   cup brown sugar, firmly packed
¼   cup butter or margarine, softened

½   cup all-purpose flour, presifted
¾   cup pecans, finely chopped
½   teaspoon vanilla extract

Preheat oven to 325°F, and line cookie sheets with foil.

In a small saucepan, combine syrup, sugar and butter. Cook over medium heat, stirring constantly, until mixture comes to a boil. Take care not to scorch.

Remove from heat, and add flour and nuts. Mix until well-blended. Add vanilla extract and mix well.

Drop onto foiled cookie sheets by teaspoonfuls, about 3 inches apart. Bake 8 to 10 minutes until golden brown.

Cool pan on wire rack. When cookies are thoroughly cooled, peel cookies off foil. Store in airtight containers.

CHAPTER

4

Golde's
One, Two, Three Cookies

I call these One, Two, Three Cookies for two reasons. The first is that most of these recipes are very easy; the only tricky part is planning your time, and even that can be quite flexible. They really are as easy as one, two, three.

The second reason is that all of these recipes call for chilling the batter or dough for at least one hour, or as long as overnight. So there are three steps: a time for preparing batter; a time to chill batter; a time to bake cookies. Each step takes very little time, and when all is said and done (if you plan your baking around your natural schedule and not the other way around), these cookies seem to prepare themselves. Though I've said it before, it's especially pertinent to these recipes . . . plan your time ahead!

FLEXIBILITY PLUS!

These recipes have a great deal of flexibility in them, so take advantage of that. In fact, most every recipe here can be started in your spare time and completed when it suits your schedule. Once your dough is prepared, you have the option of

- chilling your dough for specified time in the refrigerator and then baking;
- wrapping it *well* in plastic wrap, and refrigerating overnight or even for a few days;
- wrapping dough with freezer wrap, and freezing for as long as a month or two.

As you can see, these recipes are time-efficient for even the busiest schedules.

GOLDE'S PREPARE NOW . . . BAKE LATER METHOD

My family teases me because I take organization so seriously, but for me it makes baking easier and more enjoyable. I say that I simply never leave anything to chance, that good organization results in better prepared cookies and eliminates costly errors.

Since I usually bake in the morning I get *everything* ready the night before. For you, it might mean getting things ready when you first get home in the late afternoon, so you can bake later that night or the next evening.

Here's what I do in preparation:
- read recipe through completely
- take all ingredients out
- take out all pans, and utensils I'll need
- measure dry ingredients such as sugar or flour
- group (in the refrigerator) all other ingredients I'll be using
- put out on counter any ingredients used for decoration or garnishes

Now I'm set to go first thing in the morning. Preparation time is reduced and so are errors. I put everything away as I use it. If I need 1 teaspoon vanilla extract, the bottle goes back into the cupboard as soon as I add the teaspoonful to the batter. That way I never put an ingredient in twice, and never omit it entirely.

I urge everyone who can't find the time to bake cookies to try this "prepare-ahead . . . bake-later" method on a basic refrigerator cookie. You'll see it really works!

Cinnamon Crescents

My husband, David's, favorites. These take a little extra effort, but it's well worth it for these pastry-like cookies. Good for breakfast or brunch, too!

Preparation time: 15 minutes
Refrigerate: 3 hours

Pastry:
1   package (¼ oz.) dry yeast
¼   cup water, lukewarm
3   cups flour, sifted

2½   tablespoons granulated sugar
1   cup (2 sticks) butter or margarine, softened
2   eggs, lightly beaten

Melt butter. Beat the two eggs.

In a large bowl, sprinkle the yeast on the warm water and stir to dissolve.

Add the sifted flour. Add the sugar, melted butter and beaten eggs. Mix until well-blended.

Cover the bowl tightly and refrigerate for 3 hours or overnight. (The dough can be stored up to 3 days in the refrigerator.)

Final preparation time: 1 hour
Pan: cookie sheet, ungreased
Oven: 350°F. for 15 minutes
Yield: 48 cookies

Filling:
½   cup granulated sugar

1   tablespoon ground
    cinnamon

When ready to bake, preheat oven to 350°F.

Mix the sugar and cinnamon together and set aside.

Divide the pastry dough into 6- or 7 parts.

Take an 8- or 9-inch pie pan, and sprinkle it well with some of the filling mixture. Roll out one part of dough and press into pie pan. Sprinkle generously again with filling mixture.

Cut dough into 8 wedges, as you would a pie. Roll each wedge starting at widest end, as you would a crescent roll.

Let crescents stand 15 minutes before baking. Then place on ungreased cookie sheet, and bake for 15 minutes or until lightly golden. Remove cookies to cool on wire racks.

Repeat until all 6 or 7 dough balls are used. These freeze very well.

Variation: Before rolling into crescents, spread your favorite jam sparingly, or finely chopped nuts, or chopped raisins onto pastry dough, along with the sugar-cinnamon filling mixture.

Rolling cresents

Mrs. Vincent's Snickerdoodles

A favorite of all my daughters because Mrs. Vincent always let them feast on these cinnamon gems – fresh out of the oven.

Preparation time: 20 minutes | **Refrigeration:** 2 hours

2¾	cups all-purpose flour	1	cup vegetable shortening, softened
2	teaspoons cream of tartar		
1	teaspoon baking soda	1½	cups granulated sugar
½	teaspoon salt	2	eggs

In a large bowl, sift together flour, cream of tartar, baking soda and salt.

Cream shortening, sugar and eggs until light and fluffy. (Use electric mix master on medium speed or cream with spoon.)

Beat flour mixture (at low speed) into creamed ingredients until a dough-like batter forms. Chill for two hours, until easy to handle.

Final preparation time: 15 minutes   **Oven:** 400°F. for 8 to 10 minutes
Pan: cookie sheet, ungreased   **Yield:** 60 cookies

Topping:

2	tablespoons granulated sugar	2	teaspoons ground cinnamon

Preheat oven to 400°F.

Form dough into walnut-sized balls. Roll in topping mixture of sugar and cinnamon. Place balls 2-inches apart on ungreased cookie sheet. Bake 8 to 10 minutes or until lightly colored. Remove cookies to cool.

These are especially good when baked fresh to take advantage of the wonderful aroma and the chewy texture. But you can freeze them if you wish.

Favorite Peanut Butter Cookies

Peanut butter cookies are the unheralded but much-loved favorites of many, many people.

Preparation time: 15 minutes
Refrigerate: 1 hour or longer

1	cup brown sugar, packed	2	cups all-purpose flour
1	cup granulated sugar	1	teaspoon salt
1	cup butter or margarine, softened	1	teaspoon baking soda
1	cup peanut butter	1	teaspoon baking powder
2	eggs	1	teaspoon vanilla extract

In a large bowl, cream together the brown sugar, granulated sugar, butter, peanut butter and eggs until well-blended.

Sift the dry ingredients and add to the creamed batter. Add the vanilla extract. Mix well. Chill dough thoroughly.

Final preparation time: 15 minutes
Pan: cookie sheet, greased
Oven: 350°F. for 10 to 12 minutes
Yield: 95 cookies

When ready to bake, preheat oven to 350°F.

Break dough into walnut-sized pieces. Press these with a fork onto greased cookie sheet.

Bake for 10 to 12 minutes. Remove to wire rack and cool. These freeze very well.

Mock Streudel Slices

A light pastry bursting with apricots, raisins, nuts and coconut.
This is easier than it looks and oh-so-delicious!

Preparation time: 5 minutes
Refrigerate: overnight

Pastry:

1   cup (2 sticks) butter or
     margarine, softened

1½   cups all-purpose flour
½   cup sour cream

In a medium bowl, cut the butter into the flour until mixed and crumbly. Stir in the sour cream until blended. Divide the dough into four equal parts. Wrap each in waxed paper or plastic wrap. Refrigerate overnight or several days.

Final preparation time: 10 minutes
Pan: 15″ × 10″ jelly-roll pan, greased
Oven: 350°F. for 20 to 25 minutes
Yield: 32 pieces

Fruit Coconut Filling:

1   jar (10 oz.) apricot
     preserves
½   cup white seedless raisins

½   cup walnuts, chopped
½   cup flaked coconut
⅓   cup powdered sugar, sifted

When ready to bake, preheat oven to 350°F.

Roll the pastry dough (one at a time) out onto a well-floured board into a rectangular shape, about 11″ × 7″.

Spread with ¼ of the apricot preserves. Sprinkle with raisins, nuts and coconut.

Turn up three times as you would a jelly-roll, starting from the bottom and rolling over. Place on a greased jelly roll pan (2 streudels to a pan), and bake for 20 to 25 minutes until lightly golden. Remove pan to wire rack and cool for 5 minutes before slicing into 1-inch slices. When slices are cool, sprinkle with sifted powdered sugar. These freeze very well.

Turning up Mock Streudel Dough

Streudel Fillings

Date Filling

3	cups diced dates	1½	cups water
¼	cup granulated sugar		Lemon juice to taste

Mix all ingredients together in a saucepan.

Cook over low heat, stirring constantly, until thickened (about 10 minutes).

Cool. Proceed to fill pastry.

This may be made 2 or 3 days in advance. Keep refrigerated.

Orange-Prune Streudel Filling

3	cups steamed or cooked prunes, diced and drained		Grated rind and juice of ½ lemon
¼	to ½ cup granulated sugar	2	tablespoons grated orange rind
½	cup orange juice		

Mix all ingredients together in a saucepan. Cook over low heat, stirring constantly until thickened, about 10 minutes.

Cool thoroughly. Proceed to spread over pastry.

This may be made 2 or 3 days before using. Keep refrigerated.

Pecan Tarts

The light cream cheese pastry and pecan filling make this tart superb. These are perfect served on a tray to pass at dessert time – especially if you are serving fresh fruit, sherbet or ice cream.

Preparation time: 5 minutes   **Refrigerate:** 1 hour

Pastry:

1 small (3 oz.) package of cream cheese	½ cup butter, softened
	1 cup flour

Blend butter and cream cheese together. Then add flour, and mix until dough is formed. Chill in refrigerator at least 1 hour.

Final preparation time: 40 minutes   **Oven:** 325°F. for 25 minutes
Pan: small tart tins, ungreased   **Yield:** 24 tarts

Filling:

¾ cup brown sugar	1 tablespoon butter
1 teaspoon vanilla extract	Dash of salt
1 egg	⅔ cup pecans, coarsely chopped

When ready to bake, preheat oven to 325°F.

Shape refrigerated pastry dough into 24 1-inch balls (walnut-sized). Place in small ungreased tart tins (no paper liners). Press dough around bottom and sides.

Beat all filling ingredients (except pecans) together until smooth.

Place ⅓ cup of pecans on top of pressed pastry dough. Add 1 tablespoon of filling to each tart cup. Sprinkle remaining ⅓ cup of pecans over filling. Bake for 25 minutes until set

Remove and cool on wire rack. These freeze well, although they are somewhat delicate and need to be packed carefully.

Golde's Basic Butter Refrigerator Cookies

A sweet cookie batter which is ideal for adding nuts, fruits, chocolate pieces – make ahead, bake later!

Preparation time: 10 minutes   **Refrigerate:** about 3 hours or longer

½   cup butter, softened
1   cup granulated sugar
1   egg, beaten
1¾ cups all-purpose flour
2   teaspoons baking powder
¼   teaspoon salt

1   teaspoon vanilla extract
¾   cup chopped nuts, raisins, dates, chocolate pieces, sunflower seeds or coconut (optional)

In a large bowl, cream together the butter and sugar. Add the beaten egg. Sift the flour, baking powder and salt together. Beat the flour mixture into the creamed mixture. Add vanilla extract and any optional of ingredients you choose.

Shape the dough into two rolls, 2-inches thick and about 12-inches long. Wrap each in plastic wrap or waxed paper and refrigerate until well-chilled (or wrap in freezer wrap and freeze up to 3 months).

Final preparation time: 5 minutes   **Oven:** 375°F. for 8 to 10 minutes
Pans: cookie sheet, lightly greased   **Yield:** 96 cookies

When ready to bake, preheat oven to 375°F.

Cut rolls into thin (about ⅛-inch) slices, and bake on lightly greased cookie sheets for about 8 to 10 minutes or until golden brown. Remove cookies to cool on wire racks.

You can freeze these after baking, as well as before baking.

Brown Sugar Refrigerator Cookies

This dough can be made in advance and frozen in 2-inch × 12-inch rolls for the quickest homemade cookies ever.

Preparation time: 15 minutes   **Refrigerate:** 3 hours

1 cup butter or margarine, softened	2 cups all-purpose flour
½ cup brown sugar, packed	½ teaspoon baking soda
½ cup granulated sugar	½ teaspoon vanilla extract
1 egg, beaten slightly	½ cup nuts, chopped

In a large bowl, cream the butter, brown sugar, and granulated sugar. Add the beaten egg. Sift the flour and baking soda together. Add sifted flour to the creamed mixture; then add the vanilla and nuts.

Shape the dough with your hands into 2-inch thick rolls, about 12-inches long.

Refrigerate rolls for several hours, or wrap in freezer wrap and freeze for future baking.

Final preparation time: 5 minutes   **Oven:** 375°F. for 8 to 10 minutes
Pan: cookie sheet, greased   **Yield:** 96 cookies

When ready to bake, preheat oven to 375°F.

Slice into ¼-inch thick slices, and place on lightly greased cookie sheet. Bake for 8 to 10 minutes until golden. Remove cookies to wire rack to cool.

These freeze well after baking, too, but pack gently as very breakable.

Serving suggestion: Break these into small pieces and sprinkle over ice cream. Makes a nice homemade topping.

Coconut-Sesame Refrigerator Cookies

A light cookie flavored with sesame seed, along with a hint of almond and coconut.

Preparation time: 25 minutes
Refrigerate: 3 hours

1 cup (2 sticks) butter or margarine, softened	¾ cup flaked coconut
¾ cups granulated sugar	¼ cup almonds, finely chopped
1½ cups all-purpose flour	¼ teaspoon almond extract
¾ cup sesame seeds, lightly toasted	Dash salt

Cream the butter in a large bowl. Gradually add the sugar, beating until fluffy. Mix in the flour until well-blended.

Stir in all of the remaining ingredients.

Divide dough into thirds. Roll into 2″ × 12″ logs and wrap tightly with waxed paper or plastic wrap. Refrigerate 3 hours or freeze.

Final preparation time: 5 minutes
Pan: cookie sheet, ungreased
Oven: 300°F. for 30 minutes
Yield: 30 cookies

When ready to bake, preheat oven to 300°F.

Cut logs into slices about ¼-inch thick. Bake on ungreased cookie sheets for 30 minutes. Remove lightly browned cookies to wire rack to cool. Freeze well but be sure to layer with waxed paper.

Mincemeat Refrigerator Cookies

Here's an easy refrigerator cookie that captures the pungent flavor of mincemeat. Serve these with rice pudding, vanilla custard or ice cream.

Preparation time: 40 minutes   **Refrigerate:** 3 hours or overnight

¾	cup butter	¾	cup prepared mincemeat
1	cup granulated sugar	3	cups flour, sifted
1	egg	½	teaspoon baking soda
½	teaspoon vanilla extract	½	teaspoon salt
1	teaspoon grated lemon peel	1	teaspoon ground cinnamon
		¾	cup nuts, chopped

In a large bowl, cream together the butter and sugar, until fluffy. Beat in the egg, vanilla extract and lemon peel. Stir in the mincemeat and set aside.

Sift the flour, baking soda, salt and cinnamon together. Gradually add the sifted dry ingredients to the creamed mixture. Mix well. Stir in the nuts.

Divide the dough in half. Place each half on a sheet of waxed paper and roll to about 12 inches long. Wrap rolls in the waxed paper, and refrigerate several hours or as long as 2 to 3 days.

Final preparation time: 5 minutes   **Oven:** 375°F. for 10 minutes
Pan: cookie sheets, ungreased   **Yield:** 100 cookies

When ready to bake, preheat oven to 375°F.

Slice rolls into ⅛-inch slices and place on ungreased cookie sheets, about 2 inches apart. Bake for 10 minutes. Remove cookies to wire racks to cool.

Syl's Yeast Rugelah

The rich filling with a hint of almond puts these cookies into a class of their own! This is a very impressive cookie – always popular – and its crescent shape adds interest to any platter of cookies.

Preparation time: 20 minutes
Refrigerate: 3 hours

Pastry:

½ cup sour cream
1 tablespoon boiling water
1 package (¼ oz.) dry yeast
1 cup butter or margarine, softened

¾ cup all-purpose flour, sifted
2 egg yolks (reserve the whites for filling)
1¾ cups all-purpose flour, sifted

In a small bowl, sprinkle yeast on water, and stir until dissolved. Add sour cream, and mix. Let stand for 3 minutes.

Place softened butter and ½ cup flour in a large bowl. Add sour cream mixture and beat all together for 1 minute at low speed.

Add egg yolks, and an additional ¼ cup flour. Beat for 1 minute at medium speed. Stir in the remaining 1¾ cups flour until a soft dough forms.

Turn dough onto a floured board and knead for 8 to 10 minutes. Divide into 6 balls, and refrigerate for 3 hours (or up to 5 days).

Final preparation time: 1 hour
Pan: cookie sheet, ungreased
Oven: 375°F. for 15 to 20 minutes
Yield: 48 crescent cookies

Filling:

1 cup almonds (or other nuts), chopped	1 teaspoon vanilla extract
½ cup granulated sugar	1 teaspoon almond extract
	2 egg whites, stiffly beaten

When ready to bake, preheat oven to 375°F.

In a medium bowl, combine the filling ingredients, folding in the stiffly beaten egg whites last.

Roll as in *Cinnamon Crescents* (page 84) placing filling on top of dough only.

Let stand 15 minutes before baking. Bake on ungreased cookie sheet for 20 minutes or until golden. Remove cookies to cool on wire rack. These freeze very well.

Kneading the Rugelah Dough

Jasper Sour Cream Cookies

This is a good cookie-cutter recipe, which I have been baking for over 40 years now.

Preparation time: 15 minutes   **Refrigerate:** 3 hours

4	cups all-purpose flour	2	eggs
1	teaspoon baking soda	1	cup sour cream
1	teaspoon baking powder	1	teaspoon vanilla extract
1	cup vegetable shortening	1	cup chopped dates or raisins
1¾	cups granulated sugar		
½	teaspoon salt		

In a large bowl, sift together flour, baking soda, and baking powder. Set aside.

In a large bowl, cream together the shortening and sugar. Mix in the salt and eggs. Add the sour cream and sifted dry ingredients alternately. Mix in the vanilla extract, and lastly the dates and raisins.

Chill dough for about 3 hours or overnight.

Final preparation time: 35 minutes   **Oven:** 425°F. for 6 to 8 minutes
Pan: cookie sheets, greased   **Yield:** 96 cookies

When ready to bake, preheat oven to 425°F.

Roll out dough on well-floured surface. Cut into shapes with cookie cutters, or the rim of a glass.

Bake on greased cookie sheet for 6 to 8 minutes. Remove cookies to wire rack to cool. A good freezer cookie.

Variation: Sprinkle with colored sugar crystals before baking, or frost with *No-Fuss Cookie Frosting*.

No-Fuss Cookie Frosting

Most cookies don't need a frosting; they taste better and look inviting without a frosted surface. But sometimes – especially for holidays or birthday parties – you want that extra hint of sweetness and color. Here's the perfect frosting.

Preparation time: 15 minutes

1 cup powdered sugar, sifted	1½ tablespoons cream
¼ teaspoon salt	3 drops food coloring (optional)
½ teaspoon vanilla extract (or other flavoring, such as almond or mint)	Grated orange or lemon rind (optional)

Blend all ingredients until smooth, adding just enough cream to spread easily.

Spread on cookies with small spatula. Decorate with colored sugar crystals or chocolate sprinkles if desired.

Note: This frosting works well on *Sugar Cookies, Honey Raisin Cookies, Orange-Sour Cream Cut-Out Cookies, Jasper Sour Cream Cookies* and *Butter Delights*.

Orange-Sour Cream Cut-Out Cookies

Make this batter the night before you plan to bake these very rich cookies. This is a good one to bake with kids using cookie cutters. Frost when cool.

Preparation time: 30 minutes
Refrigerate: overnight

1 cup butter or margarine, softened	1 teaspoon baking powder
1¼ cups granulated sugar	1 cup sour cream
2 eggs	Grated rind of 1 orange
3¼ cups all-purpose flour	(about 2 teaspoons)

In a large bowl, cream the butter and 1¼ cups granulated sugar together.

Add the eggs one at a time, beating thoroughly after each addition.

Sift flour and baking powder together. Alternating with the sour cream, add flour mixture to the creamed mixture. Blend very well and add orange rind.

Wrap tightly and chill overnight.

Final preparation time: 50 minutes
Pan: cookie sheet, greased
Oven: 375°F. for 12 minutes
Yield: 96 cookies

Topping:

⅓   cup granulated sugar   ⅓   cup almonds, finely chopped

Preheat oven to 375°F.

Turn dough out on floured board, and roll or press to ¼-inch thickness. Cut cookies with cookie cutters, or the rim of a 2-inch wide glass.

Combine the chopped almonds and sugar; sprinkle on cookies.

Bake on greased baking sheet for 10 to 12 minutes. Remove cookies to wire rack to cool.

Cutting out Cookies

Grandma's Brown Lace Cookies

Absolutely delicious! These are almost unbeatable – a dessert in themselves served with tea, coffee, or milk.

Preparation time: 25 minutes
Refrigerate: 1 hour or overnight

¼ cup (4 tablespoons) butter or margarine
2   cups brown sugar, packed
2   eggs, well-beaten
1   teaspoon vanilla extract

½   cup all-purpose flour
1   teaspoon baking powder
1   cup pecans, coarsely chopped

In a medium bowl, cream the butter and brown sugar. Add the beaten eggs, and beat all together until well-blended. Add the vanilla extract and mix.

Sift flour and baking powder together. Mix in the chopped nuts.

Gradually add the flour mixture to the creamed ingredients. Mix until well-blended. Cover with waxed paper and refrigerate at least one hour.

Final preparation time: 10 minutes
Pans: cookie sheets, greased and floured
Oven: 400°F. for 6 to 8 minutes
Yield: 30 cookies

When ready to bake, preheat oven to 400°F.

Remove dough from refrigerator. Grease cookie sheets and then sprinkle with flour. Drop dough by ½ teaspoonfuls, about 3 inches apart onto cookie sheets. Bake for 6 to 8 minutes.

Remove from pan when *slightly* cooled, to wire racks.

These are very delicate so freeze carefully.

Pineapple Drops

This cookie has a cake-like texture and is not too sweet. A nice cookie for mid-morning snack at school, office, or home.

Preparation time: 20 to 25 minutes
Refrigerate: at least 1 hour

1 cup vegetable shortening	3½ cups all-purpose flour, sifted
2 cups granulated sugar	1 teaspoon baking soda
1 egg	½ teaspoon salt
1 can (8 oz.) crushed pineapple with liquid	¼ teaspoon ground nutmeg
	½ cup nuts, chopped

In a large bowl, beat together shortening, sugar and egg. Mix in the pineapple with liquid.

Sift the flour, baking soda, salt, and nutmeg together. Add to creamed mixture. Stir in nuts.

Chill batter at least 1 hour.

Final preparation time: 10 minutes
Pan: cookie sheets, greased
Oven: 400°F. for 8 to 10 minutes
Yield: 72 cookies

When ready to bake, preheat oven to 400°F.

Drop batter by teaspoonfuls on greased cookie sheet. Bake for 8 to 10 minutes or until no imprint remains when touched lightly.

Remove cookies to wire rack to cool. These freeze well.

Variation: For a sweeter cookie, sprinkle with sifted powdered sugar while still warm.

Ginger Snaps

Sprinkle 2 to 3 drops of water on unbaked cookies to get that traditional crinkled ginger snap surface.

Preparation time: 15 minutes   **Refrigerate:** 1/2 hour

¾	cup vegetable shortening	2	cups all-purpose flour
1	cup granulated sugar	1	teaspoon baking soda
1	egg	1	teaspoon ground cinnamon
¼	cup molasses	1	teaspoon ground cloves
		1	teaspoon ground ginger

In a large bowl, cream together the butter, sugar, egg and molasses until well-blended.

Sift the flour, baking soda and spices together. Add to the creamed mixture. Mix until thoroughly blended.

Wrap and refrigerate dough for ½ hour.

Final preparation time: 10 minutes
Pan: cookie sheets, greased
Oven: 375°F. for 10 to 12 minutes
Yield: 84 cookies

Topping:
⅓   cup granulated sugar

When ready to bake, preheat oven to 375°F.

In your hands, roll dough into balls about half-teaspoon size. Dip each ball into sugar topping. Place on greased cookie sheet about 2-inches apart. Sprinkle 2 to 3 drops of water on each cookie. Bake for 10 to 12 minutes. Remove dark brown cookies to cool on wire rack. These freeze very well.

CHAPTER

5

Golde's Fun and Festive Cookies

A variety of cookies – some molded, some shaped, some simply formed into a ball – but all quite simple to bake, and pretty to look at. Many of these recipes are perfect for baking with children.

BAKING WITH CHILDREN

Kids – both boys and girls – have a wonderful time baking. It's one of those activities where grown-ups, young children, and teenagers can all share in a creative effort, and then delight in the outcome. Baking with children can be as creative as you like, as personal as you want, humorous or serious, precise or not – whatever environment you create.

Depending on the age of the children, you may want to have the batter partially prepared. Older children, though, will want to make the batter from scratch. Some children may only need to stir a few times before shaping the batter; little ones may be thrilled to pick and choose garnishes for already formed cookies (try *Jewel's Cookies* for the youngest ones). Use your judgment as to what your particular group is capable of doing, and prepare everything up to that point *before* they join you.

TEACHING WHILE YOU BAKE

It's never too early (or too late, for that matter) to teach children the rudiments of good baking. I used to teach the local Girl Scout troops their Baking Badge, and years later some of the, now grown, women stop by to say they still follow my instructions.
- Emphasize reading the recipe before you start.
- Assemble all ingredients and explain what they are used for, such as baking soda as a leavening.
- Demonstrate how to properly measure liquids (in a glass measuring cup, on a flat surface) and dry ingredients (in graduated measuring cups, levelled with a knife).

- Stress to never measure over the batter bowl in case of a spill.
- Teach the children all about eggs. How to crack them and how to separate them (again not over the batter bowl). How to mix them slightly or beat them to a yellow foam. How to beat egg whites and *fold* them in.
- Encourage children to get "into" the cookie-making process. Try to avoid fussing about spills, but rather encourage their natural spontaneity and clever ideas. Your kitchen will be chaotic, but the positive baking experience will last for many, many years.
- If possible, choose a recipe that has fun built into it. (See list, Chapter 7.) Provide a wide assortment of cookie cutters, garnishes, colored sugar crystals, fillings, and let their imaginations run wild. You'll be amazed at what they think of – some cookies will be loaded down with everything, others will be sparsely decorated.
- Teach subtly and quietly, more by example than by correcting what they do. Keep conversation flowing, asking what they are making, gently explaining what you are doing. Give lots of praise and encouragement.
- Assign everyone a small clean-up task, so that, too, becomes part of the overall experience.
- Share the fruits of their labor, both by admiring the freshly baked cookies, eating some all together, and giving everyone a few to take home.
- Most importantly, really enjoy the time you spend baking with children. Listen to what they say, acknowledge their ideas and cookie creations. They'll respond so warmly that you'll be smiling for a long time to come. It really is a special time together.

Poppy Seed-Lemon Cookies

You can either make these with a cookie press in interesting shapes, cut with cookie cutters, or simply roll them. Either way, these are delicate cookies with the subtle flavors of poppy seeds and lemon.

Preparation time: 25 minutes
Pan: cookie sheet, greased
Oven: 400°F. for 8 to 10 minutes
Yield: 50 cookies

½ cup (1 stick) butter or margarine, softened	⅓ cup poppy seeds
½ cup granulated sugar	1½ cups all-purpose flour
1 egg, beaten	1 teaspoon lemon juice
1 teaspoon baking powder	½ teaspoon lemon rind, grated
¼ teaspoon salt	

Preheat oven to 400°F.

In a large bowl, cream the butter and sugar together. Add the beaten egg and mix well. Set aside.

Sift the flour, baking powder and salt together.

Gradually add the flour to the creamed mixture and blend well. Add the poppy seeds. Flavor with lemon juice and rind.

If using cookie press, fill and press onto greased cookie sheet. Or roll out dough on floured board until quite thin, and cut with cookie cutters or with the rim of a 2-inch glass.

Bake for 8 to 10 minutes. Remove cookies and cool on wire racks.

Jewel's Cookies

My grandchildren always ask to bake these with me – it's a perfect recipe to use with children!

Preparation time: 20 minutes
Pan: cookie sheet, lightly greased
Oven: 350°F. for 25 minutes
Yield: 36 cookies

Pastry:
2   cups all-purpose flour
1   cup (2 sticks) butter or margarine, softened
½   cup granulated sugar
2   egg yolks

Filling:
1   jar of jam or preserves, maraschino cherries, glazed fruit, nuts, or chocolate kisses

Preheat oven to 350°F.

In a large bowl, mix all of the pastry ingredients together until well-blended.

Break off walnut-sized pieces of dough and roll into balls. Flatten each ball in its center with your thumb and fill with whatever you choose – jams and cherries look pretty. A variety of fillings make an attractive assortment.

Bake on lightly greased cookie sheets for 25 minutes. Remove cookies to wire rack to cool.

Variation: This cookie is an ideal choice if you want to tint some cookies a pale pink. Just add 2 to 3 drops of red food coloring to batter.

Molasses 'N Spice Cookies

A rich, dark, spicy cookie that is especially nice to serve in the deep winter months.

Preparation time: 25 minutes
Pan: cookie sheet, ungreased
Oven: 375°F. for 10 minutes
Yield: 60 cookies

2	cups all-purpose flour	1	cup granulated sugar
1	teaspoon baking soda	¼	teaspoon salt
1	teaspoon ground ginger	1	egg, beaten
1	teaspoon ground cloves	¼	cup molasses
1	teaspoon ground cinnamon		
¾	cups vegetable shortening, melted		

Preheat oven to 375°F.

Sift the flour, baking soda and spices together. Set aside.

In a large bowl, cool melted shortening. Add sugar, salt, egg and molasses. Then, add sifted ingredients. Mix until well-blended.

Form walnut-sized balls, place on ungreased cookie sheets, and press flat with back of fork.

Bake for 10 minutes. Remove cookies to wire racks to cool.

Butter Delights

These are almost as light and buttery as shortbread cookies, and much easier to make!

Preparation time: 15 minutes
Pan: cookie sheet, greased
Oven: 375°F. for 15 minutes
Yield: 36 cookies

1½ cups all-purpose flour, sifted	½ cup granulated sugar
½ cup cornstarch	1 cup (2 sticks) sweet butter or margarine, softened

Preheat oven to 375°F.

In a medium bowl, mix all ingredients together until well-blended.

Break off walnut-sized pieces. Roll into balls and flatten each with the back of a fork (so fork lines show).

Bake on a greased cookie sheet for 13 to 15 minutes or until lightly browned. Remove cookies to wire rack to cool.

Variation: If you have small butter molds, try pressing these against cookies to create interesting designs.

Variation: *Butter Delights* are perfect for adding a drop or two of red or green food coloring to final batter. Sprinkle with red or green sugar crystals when almost cool or roll balls in sugar crystals before baking.

Confetti Date Balls

These are a visual treat, as well as a rich-tasting confection. Perfect for gift tins, as well as in small candy dishes.

Preparation time: 20 minutes
Pan: cookie sheet, greased
Oven: 350°F. for 12 to 15 minutes
Yield: 36 cookies

1 (8 oz.) package dates	1 cup brown sugar, firmly packed
1 teaspoon water	2 egg whites, beaten stiff
1 tablespoon butter	1 cup shredded coconut
1 cup walnuts, coarsely chopped	

Preheat oven to 350°F.

In a small saucepan, soften the dates in the butter, along with about ½ teaspoon of water. Cook over very low heat, and watch carefully, stirring to prevent scorching (or soften in double boiler).

In a medium bowl, combine softened dates with the brown sugar and chopped nuts. Fold in the stiffly beaten egg whites.

Form into walnut-sized balls, and roll each ball in the coconut. Bake on greased cookie sheets for 12 to 15 minutes, until lightly browned.

Cool date balls on wire rack. These freeze very well.

Chocolate Crackles

Enjoy these luscious chocolate treats . . . and try not to eat them all at one sitting!

Preparation time: 35 minutes
Pan: cookie sheet, lined with foil

Oven: 350°F. for 12 to 14 minutes
Yield: 96 cookies

3 cups all-purpose flour	2 tablespoons water
1¼ teaspoons baking soda	2 cups (12 oz.) semisweet chocolate pieces
½ teaspoon salt	
1½ cups dark brown sugar, packed	2 eggs
¾ cups butter or margarine, softened	½ cup granulated sugar (optional)

Preheat oven to 350°F.

Sift the flour, baking soda, and salt together. Set aside.

In a large saucepan, cook the butter, brown sugar and water, stirring until the butter melts. Add the chocolate pieces, stirring until the chocolate is almost melted. Remove from heat and stir until chocolate is completely melted. Transfer chocolate mixture to a large bowl and let cool slightly (5 minutes).

Beat eggs one at a time into chocolate mixture with electric mixer on high speed. Reduce speed, and gradually add sifted dry ingredients. Let batter set until dough can be handled (about 10 minutes; don't refrigerate).

Line a cookie sheet with aluminum foil. Roll dough into walnut-sized balls, about 20 balls to a cookie sheet. You can roll each ball in granulated sugar before baking, if you choose.

Bake for 12 to 14 minutes. Tops will feel dry, but not firm. The cookies will crisp as they cool on wire racks. These freeze very well.

Golden Nuggets

These are a favorite cookie because they are so versatile – fill them with whatever you have on hand, or roll them in colorful sugar crystals.

Preparation time: 25 minutes
Pan: cookie sheet, greased

Oven: 325°F. for 25 to 30 minutes
Yield: 36 cookies

1   cup (2 sticks) butter or
    margarine, softened
½   cup granulated sugar
1   egg yolk, unbeaten
1   teaspoon grated orange
    rind
2½ cups all-purpose flour, sifted

Filling:
Dates, nuts, jam, maraschino cherries, chocolate pieces, or any other filling of your choice
Powdered sugar, sifted

Preheat oven to 325°F.

In a large bowl, cream together the butter and sugar. Add the egg yolk and rind, blending well.

Mix in the flour, forming a heavy dough.

Take a walnut-sized piece of dough and flatten in your hand. Fill center with filling of your choice, and shape dough around it; roll into a ball. Place on greased cookie sheet, and bake 25 to 30 minutes. Nuggets will be quite light in color even when they are done.

Remove nuggets to wire rack, and sprinkle with powdered sugar while still hot.

These freeze well, but wait to sprinkle with powdered sugar after defrosting.

Variation: For special treats, add 1 or 2 drops (no more) of pink food coloring to the dough. They look very festive with the powdered sugar. Or before baking, roll in colorful crystals, confetti sprinkles, or cinnamon sugar.

No-Bake Rum Balls

A no-bake confection that can be served as you would chocolate truffles with after-dinner coffee.

Preparation time: 15 minutes
Pan: store in covered tin
Oven: no baking
Yield: 36 balls

2½ cups vanilla wafers, crushed	1 cup walnuts, chopped
2 tablespoons cocoa	3 tablespoons dark corn syrup
1 cup powdered sugar	¼ cup rum (or brandy)

In a medium bowl, mix all ingredients together in the order listed.

When well-blended, form into walnut-sized balls. Roll balls in additional powdered sugar.

Store in covered tin.

Mocha Nut Cookies

A mild flavored tea cookie that's not too sweet. A nice late-evening snack with tea or milk.

Preparation time: 25 minutes
Pan: cookie sheet, greased
Oven: 325°F. for 13 to 15 minutes
Yield: 48 cookies

1	cup butter or margarine, softened	1¾	cups all-purpose flour, sifted
½	cup granulated sugar	½	teaspoon salt
2	teaspoons vanilla extract	2	cups nuts, finely chopped
1	egg yolk	⅓	cup powdered sugar
¼	cup cocoa		

Preheat oven to 325°F.

In a large bowl, cream together the butter, sugar, and vanilla. When well-blended, add the egg yolk and mix.

Sift together the cocoa, flour, and salt. Add the creamed mixture. Mix batter well. Add the nuts.

Shape dough into walnut-sized balls, and place on a greased cookie sheet. Bake for 13 to 15 minutes. Remove to a wire rack. Roll in powdered sugar when almost cool.

Variation: Substitute 1½ cups shredded coconut for chopped nuts.

Pecan Butter Balls

Wonderfully simple . . . simply wonderful!

Preparation time: 20 minutes
Pan: cookie sheets, greased
Oven: 300°F. for 30 minutes
Yield: 30 cookies

½ cup butter or margarine, softened	1 cup pecans, finely chopped
2 tablespoons sugar	1 cup all-purpose flour, sifted
1 teaspoon vanilla extract	Powdered sugar

Preheat oven to 300°F.

Beat the butter until creamy. Add the sugar and vanilla extract, and continue to beat well. Stir in the chopped pecans and sifted flour.

Roll small pieces of dough into small balls, and bake for 30 minutes.

While still hot, roll balls in powdered sugar.

Return to oven for 1 minute so cookies will form glaze.

Remove to wire rack to cool.

These freeze very well.

Pecan Fingers

Sweet, chewy, and attractive, with the added bonus of being very easy to make, too!

Preparation time: 20 minutes
Pan: cookie sheets, greased
Oven: 325°F. for 25 to 30 minutes
Yield: 48 cookies

1 cup butter	1½ cups pecans, coarsely chopped
¾ cup powdered sugar	1 tablespoon ice water
1 teaspoon vanilla extract	⅛ teaspoon salt
2 cups flour, sifted	Powdered sugar

Preheat oven to 325°F.

In a medium bowl, cream the butter and powdered sugar together. Add the remaining ingredients, and mix well.

Break off small pieces of dough and roll with palm of hands into finger lengths.

Bake for 25 to 30 minutes. Remove from oven to cool on wire racks. While still slightly warm, roll each cookie in additional powdered sugar.

These freeze well. They look freshest when rolled in powdered sugar after defrosting. (Heat slightly in oven before rolling.)

CHAPTER

6

Golde's Specialty Cookies

Many of the recipes in this chapter are personal favorites of mine, but that is not the reason I included them here. These cookies add visual appeal to any assortment of cookies, whether served at home or packaged for a gift.

And visual appeal is well worth considering in any cookie presentation. Sometimes of course, there is nothing better than a plate piled high with one kind of cookie. Certainly *Chocolate Chip Crispers* or *Zucchini Oatmeal Cookies* can be consumed in large quantities faster than you can pour milk for a cookies 'n milk snack.

But other times a more varied presentation will be effective in creating the atmosphere you want.

PRESENTATION POINTERS

- Select cookies appropriate to the occasion and setting. Will the people be sitting or standing? Some cookies are more difficult to eat without a napkin or plate.
- How do you want your platter to look – casual with cookies heaped on, or formally arranged with each cookie having a place of its own?
- For large platters, arrange all cookies of one kind together, rather than mixing them throughout. This way you achieve visual appeal, as well as avoid a mingling of flavors. Each type of cookie can make a statement.
- Will the cookies be the main dessert or are they an adjunct to another dessert?
- Select an appropriately-sized platter, tray or dish to serve your cookies on. If it looks over-crowded or too sparsely covered, people are reluctant to help themselves.

- Try using several small, unusually shaped, silver serving dishes, each with a single kind of attractive cookie, such as a small dish of *Cinnamon Crescents*, another of *Cream Puff Pastries with Strawberry Filling*, and a third dish of *Walnut Surprises*. Pass these around the dining table when coffee is served.
- Consider unusual dishes for presenting your cookies. Baskets lined with linen napkins are very festive; odd pieces of china or crystal make interesting serving pieces, as well as beautifully polished silver trays and pewter platters.
- Keep cookies covered with plastic wrap or aluminum foil until ready to serve to prevent drying out.
- Refresh frozen cookies with a sprinkling of sifted powdered sugar.

COOKIES AND . . .

It's good to stretch your imagination when it comes to serving ideas. Cookies and milk go together as well as peanut butter and jelly, but there are many other pleasing combinations.

- Serve cookies with fresh fruit cup. Just before serving, add a generous sprinkling of champagne to your fresh fruit mixture. Pass a plate of *Lemon Squares* and *Raisin Nut Tarts*.
- Try strawberries and cream with a platter of *Accordion Treats*.
- Pass a dessert cheese such as Kirsch Gourmandaise along with bunches of green and red grapes. Place a platter of *Coconut-Sesame Cookies* and *Lemony Pecan Bars* on the table's center.
- Serve a dessert coffee along with a platter of *Seafoam Chews* and *Cream Cheese Tarts*.

- Serve hot baked apples. Pass bowls of honey, whipped cream and a basket of *Spicy Fruit Cookies*.
- Try coffee ice cream topped with warm maple syrup. Pass the *Double Fudge Brownies Supreme*.
- You'll delight in homemade raspberry sherbet along with wonderful *Chinese Chews*.
- Scoop some vanilla ice cream on top of generous portions of *Pecan Pie Treasures*.
- Whenever you serve custards, puddings or souffles, place a few small dishes of cookies on the table to munch while lingering over coffee. Try *Crispy Oatmeal-Raisin Cookies, or Pecan Butter Balls*.
- Serving a heavy dessert? Pass some light cookies such as *Chocolate Thinsees, Butter Delights*, and *Poppy-Seed Lemon Cookies*.
- Serve your favorite ice cream in champagne glasses. Cover with a splash of Kahlua or Amaretto Liqueur, and crumble *Oriental Crunch* on top.

As you can see, cookies complement just about any dessert. An attractive presentation enhances your table and creates a welcoming environment.

And it's amazing how quickly a group can relax around a plate of aromatic delicious cookies. "Cookie comraderie" is a great icebreaker. Somehow cookies and friendliness go together. I tend to think that is because homebaked cookies used to say "I care about you" to us as children, and so, they still communicate affection to us as adults.

Here's to broadening your cookie experience!

Bev's Shortbread Cookies

This is a very special cookie – so rich and buttery that it seems to melt in your mouth. I always baked these with my daughters for all our neighbors at holiday time.

Preparation time: 25 minutes
Pan: cookie sheet, greased
Oven: 375°F. for 8 to 10 minutes
Yield: 70 small cookies

1	cup (2 sticks) butter, softened	½	teaspoon vanilla extract
½	cup powdered sugar		Pinch salt
2	cups all-purpose flour, sifted	2	to 3 drops red or green food coloring (optional)
			Decorative edibles (optional)

Note: This cookie can only be made with a cookie press, as they don't roll out nicely.

Preheat oven to 375°F.

In a medium bowl, cream all ingredients together until very well-blended. (Use your food processor, if you have one).

Fill cookie press, and squeeze cookies out onto greased cookie sheet. Use a variety of shapes and designs.

Bake for 8 to 10 minutes. Cookies will be very pale, slightly browned at bottom, when done. Remove cookies to wire rack to cool and decorate.

These make a wonderful tea cookie, and they freeze very well.

Variations: For colorful cookies, tint batter. Press out into varied designs. Decorate with cherries, chips and jams before baking. Decorate with sugar crystals, chocolate sprinkles or confetti sprinkles after baking, but before completely cooled.

Brandy Snaps

These lacey, delicate cookies are perfect with light fruit desserts or dessert coffees; they are an elegant embellishment to any dessert. Try them too with a dish of coffee ice cream.

Preparation time: 15 minutes
Pan: cookie sheets, greased
Oven: 375°F. for 8 to 10 minutes
Yield: 100 cookies

Shaping Brandy Snaps

1   cup brown sugar, packed
1   cup molasses
¾   cup butter, melted
2   teaspoons ground ginger
2   scant cups all-purpose flour, sifted

Preheat oven to 375°F.

In a large bowl, combine all ingredients until well-blended.

Drop by ½ teaspoonfuls onto a greased cookie sheet, leaving at least 3 inches between cookies, as these spread out quite a bit while baking.

Bake for 8 to 10 minutes, or until they are semi-crisp, lacey, and bubbly.

Remove from cookie sheet with a wide spatula, and immediately shape each cookie by rolling it, using the handle of a knife or handle of a wooden spoon before it has time to cool. Work quickly so that each can be shaped while still flexible.

These do not freeze well.

Chinese Chews

These are a family favorite – a chewy, sweet confection that goes with everything. The unusual rolled shape makes this visually appealing.

Preparation time: 15 minutes
Pan: 15″ × 10″ jelly-roll pan, greased
Oven: 350°F. for 20 to 25 minutes
Yield: 48 cookies

1   cup granulated sugar
¾   cup all-purpose flour
¼   teaspoon salt
1   teaspoon baking powder
1   cup dates, finely diced

1   cup walnuts, chopped
2   eggs

Topping:
½   cup sifted powdered sugar

Preheat oven to 350°F.

In a large bowl, sift sugar, flour, salt, and baking powder together.

Add eggs, dates and nuts. Blend until a dough forms.

Pat the dough into a greased 15″ × 10″ jelly-roll pan.

Bake for 20 to 25 minutes.

Immediately upon removal from oven, cut into 1″ × 1″ squares, and roll crust side (top) inward in powdered sugar. The squares must still be warm enough to shape while rolling.

If they cool too much, return to the oven to warm.

Chinese Chews freeze very well.

Tart Pastry

Prepare your favorite 2-crust pie pastry for Raisin Nut Tarts and Butter Tarts, or use the following pastry recipe.

Preparation time: 10 minutes; refrigerate 2 hours.
Pan: tart tins
Yield: 2-crust pastry enough for 20 small tarts

1¾ cups all-purpose flour
1   teaspoon salt
⅔   cup vegetable shortening

¼   cup very cold water
    (approximate)

In a medium bowl, mix the flour and salt. Cut in the vegetable shortening until crumbly.

Add the water, little by little, until the dough can be gathered into a ball. It shouldn't be sticky so use as little water as possible.

Refrigerate dough for at least two hours.

When thoroughly chilled, roll dough out on floured surface. Cut pastry to fill bottom and sides of small paper tart cups. Fork holes into bottom dough. Follow tart recipes.

Rum Raisin Tarts

A dark brown sugar tart with a hint of rum and plenty of raisins and nuts.

Preparation time: 30 minutes
Pan: tart tins
Oven: 375°F. for 15 to 20 minutes
Yield: 20 small tarts

Prepare enough pie pastry for a 2-crust pie (page 126).
Press pastry into small paper tart cups along the bottom and sides.
Preheat oven to 375°F.

Filling:

1½	cups seedless raisins	2	cups brown sugar, packed
4	tablespoons butter	1	cup nuts, chopped
2	eggs	2	to 3 teaspoons rum

Soak the raisins in boiling water for a few minutes until softened. Strain and set raisins aside.

In a large bowl, beat the butter at medium speed until creamy. Add the eggs and brown sugar, and beat until foamy.

Mix in the rum, nuts, and raisins.

Fill unbaked tart crusts ⅔ full. Bake for 15 to 20 minutes until brown. Remove from oven and cool tarts on wire rack.

Golden Butter Tarts

These are a delight. So light, yet also rich – that special butter-brown sugar balance.

Preparation time: 45 minutes
Pan: tart tins
Oven: 425°F. for 10 to 15 minutes
Yield: 20 small tarts

Prepare your favorite 2-crust pastry, or see page 126.
Preheat oven to 425°F.

Filling:

⅓ cup butter, melted
½ cup seedless raisins
½ cup golden corn syrup

½ cup brown sugar, packed
¼ teaspoon salt
1 egg

Melt the butter and set aside to cool. Beat egg.

In a medium bowl, mix together the melted butter and beaten egg. Add the brown sugar, salt, and syrup and continue mixing until smooth.

Line small tart cups with pastry along bottom and side. Fork holes in bottom.

Place 3 or 4 raisins in each tart cup, and spoon 1 scant teaspoon filling into each cup, leaving plenty of room for expansion.

Bake for 10 to 15 minutes on the lowest oven rack.

Remove from oven and let cool three minutes before removing from tins. Loosen edges of each tart with a knife, and continue cooling tarts on wire racks.

These freeze very well, although somewhat fragile.

Cream Cheese Tarts

If you like cheesecake, you'll love these small tarts. Smooth and creamy, they melt in your mouth. Best of all, they are easy to make and they freeze well, too.

Preparation time: 20 minutes
Pan: tart tins

Oven: 375°F. for 10 minutes
Yield: 24 small tarts

Crust:
1½ cups graham cracker crumbs
⅓ cup butter or margarine, melted

Filling:
1 lb. (16 oz.) cream cheese
2 eggs
1 teaspoon vanilla extract
½ cup granulated sugar

Preheat oven to 375°F.

Prepare crust my mixing graham cracker crumbs and melted butter together. Press about 1 tablespoon in each tart cup lined with tea papers. Set aside.

Prepare filling in a medium bowl by blending all filling ingredients together. Beat with an electric mixer for about 5 minutes.

Place a generous tablespoon of filling mixture on top of each crumb crust.

Bake for 10 minutes and remove from pan to cool on wire racks. Sprinkle a few graham cracker crumbs on top to give added color.

These freeze very well.

Variation 1: *Cinnamon Crust:* For just a hint of cinnamon in these tarts, add ¼ teaspoon ground cinnamon to crust ingredients.

Variation 2: *Raspberry Cheese Tarts:* Add ½ teaspoon of raspberry jam to each tart cup on top of crumb crust before filling with the cream cheese mixture.

Almond Brickles

My daughter, Debby, calls these "Dentist Delights." They look and taste very much like peanut brittle. These cookies take a little extra effort, but they are worth it.

Preparation time: 40 minutes
Pans: 15″ × 10″ jelly-roll pan, greased
Oven: 375°F. for 10 minutes (pastry);
        375°F. for 18 minutes (with topping)
Yield: 40 to 48 pieces

Pastry:
1¾ cups all-purpose flour
2½ tablespoons granulated
    sugar
¾   teaspoon baking powder
Dash salt
½   cup butter or margarine
1   egg, beaten
2   to 3 tablespoons milk or
    heavy cream

Preheat oven to 375°F.

Topping:
1½ cup granulated sugar
½   cup butter
½   cup heavy cream
¾   cup honey
1½ cups slivered almonds
¼   teaspoon vanilla extract

In a large bowl, thoroughly combine flour, 2½ tablespoons sugar, baking powder, and salt. Cut in ½ cup butter until mixture is crumbly. Then mix in the beaten egg. Add the milk gradually. Mix lightly until a light fluffy pastry forms. Gently pat into pan and bake at 375°F for 10 minutes.

Meanwhile, in a heavy saucepan prepare the topping by combining the sugar, butter, cream, vanilla extract, and honey. Cook over medium heat, stirring constantly. Test for doneness by dropping a small amount into cold water. When it comes out a firm but soft ball, it is ready. Pour topping over the baked pastry. Return to oven and bake 18 minutes until caramel colored. Sprinkle almonds evenly on top. Cut into squares while still warm and cool on wire rack. Or break into assorted pieces and cool. These freeze well but be sure to put waxed paper between layers.

Variation: Chopped peanuts are wonderful in this recipe, and less expensive than almonds. For baking, buy the generic unsalted peanuts which are lower priced and work just as well.

Patting Pastry into a jelly-roll pan

Favorite Mandel Broit

These mildly flavored, toast-like cookies are favorites at breakfast, lunch, or late-night snack.

Preparation time: 35 minutes
Pan: cookie sheets, greased
Oven: 375°F. loaves for 15 to 20 minutes, slices for 20 minutes more
Yield: 60 cookies

1	cup vegetable shortening	4	cups flour
1	cup granulated sugar	1	teaspoon baking powder
4	eggs	½	cup nuts, chopped
1	teaspoon vanilla extract		(optional)

Preheat oven to 375°F.

In a large bowl, cream together the shortening and granulated sugar. Add the eggs and vanilla extract. Mix well and set aside.

Sift the flour and baking powder together and add gradually to the creamed mixture. Add nuts and mix very well.

Knead the dough on a lightly floured board. Divide dough into five or six separate rolls about one inch high and 2½ to 3 inches long. Bake rolls on greased cookie sheets for 15 to 20 minutes, until browned.

Remove rolls from oven and slice into pieces, one inch wide. Place slices cut side down and bake another 20 minutes, turning slices after 10 minutes so both sides are lightly browned and crisp.

Remove slices to wire rack to cool.

Variations: You may substitute almond extract for vanilla extract. Add candied fruits instead of nuts, if you wish.

Pinwheel Pastries

A rich pastry, delicately folded into a pinwheel, filled with your favorite preserves. A very special cookie indeed!

*Preparation time: pastry: 15 minutes
                                    wheels: 30 minutes
Pan: cookie sheet, lightly greased
Oven: 375°F. for 10 to 12 minutes
Yield: 48 pinwheels   *Pastry is refrigerated overnight

1   cup (2 sticks) butter, softened
8   ounces (1 large package) cream cheese, softened

2   cups flour, sifted
1   jar favorite preserves
Walnuts, finely chopped (optional)

In a medium bowl, cream together butter and cream cheese. Add flour gradually and mix until very well-blended. Cover and refrigerate overnight.

Preheat oven to 375°F.

Roll out dough to about ⅛-inch thickness. Cut into rounds with rim of glass, about 2 inches in diameter. Place preserves (mixed with chopped nuts, if desired) in center of circle.

To shape into pinwheels, cut outer circle into fourths, leaving jam center intact. Fold ½ of each fourth over onto itself. Press folds down with top of fork.

Bake for 10 to 12 minutes until nicely browned. Remove pan from oven to cool for a minute or two, and then gently lift pinwheels off to cool on wire rack.

Variation: *Cheesey Pinwheel Pastries:* For a less sweet pastry, omit the jam filling. Instead sprinkle pastry circles with grated Parmesan Cheese. Fold into pinwheels and brush with beaten egg yolk; bake as above.

Cream Puff Pastries

These are so versatile. Fill them with whatever you have on hand – fresh fruit, whips, custards, ice cream, puddings – they always taste delicious and look elegant.

Preparation time: 25 minutes
Pan: cookie sheet, greased
Oven: 400°F. for 35 minutes
Yield: 12 medium-sized puffs

¼	cup butter	½	cup sifted all-purpose flour
½	cup boiling water	2	eggs

In a saucepan, add butter to boiling water. Continue heating until butter melts. Add the flour all at once. Stir vigorously over heat until a ball forms in center of saucepan.

Remove from heat. Add eggs, one at a time, beating the batter after each egg is added. The batter should be very stiff.

Drop by rounded tablespoonfuls onto greased cookie sheet, leaving about 1½" between puffs.

Bake for 35 minutes. Remove to wire rack to cool. When cool make a small opening ¾-way around puff, and fill with favorite filling.

If you are serving these as a cookie – to be eaten with the hands – don't overfill them. They work best with a stiffly whipped cream filling which you can delicately flavor with chocolate or liqueurs, or with a traditional creamy custard filling.

Strawberry Whipped-Cream Filling

A very light summertime dessert that's also very elegant.
Serve these on a pretty platter garnished with halved
fresh strawberries (hull still on).

Preparation time: 10 minutes
Yield: filling for 20 small puffs

1 cup chilled whipping cream	¾ cup fresh strawberries, sliced
¼ cup powdered sugar, sifted	½ teaspoon vanilla extract

Chill bowl, beaters and cream. Whip cream with sifted powdered sugar and vanilla extract until stiff.

Fold in sliced strawberries

Put a generous teaspoon of creamed filling into each puff so that filling shows between top and bottom halves of puff. Refrigerate or serve immediately.

Accordion Treats

This special recipe makes wedge-shaped, long, slim cookies.
Very elegant and very delicious, too!

Preparation time: 40 minutes   **Oven:** 325°F. for 25 to 30 minutes
Pan: cookie sheet with aluminum foil   **Yield:** 60 cookies

1	yard heavy duty aluminum foil
¾	cup butter
¾	cup granulated sugar
2	eggs
1	teaspoon vanilla extract
¼	teaspoon salt
1¼	cups flour, sifted

Preheat oven to 325°F.

To prepare foil accordion, fold 1 yard of foil lengthwise, to double thickness. Then, starting at top, fold into 1-inch accordion pleats. Pull open and place on cookie sheet or jelly-roll pan.

In large mixing bowl, cream butter. Gradually add the granulated sugar and cream very well, until light. Blend in eggs, vanilla extract and salt, and beat well. Gradually add sifted flour and mix thoroughly

Drop by *very* scant teaspoonfuls into center of folds of foil, one teaspoonful per fold. Use about one-half of the dough. The dough will spread in baking.

Bake for 25 to 30 minutes until pale golden. Remove pan to wire racks and cool for 10 minutes. Remove cookies from foil.

Shake off crumbs and reuse foil for remaining dough.

CHAPTER

7

Cookie Versatility

We all have our personal preferences in cookies – some prefer chewy instead of crisp; light, thin refrigerator cookies rather than layered, dense bar cookies. Some will eat anything with chocolate, others lean towards raisin-coconut combinations. But whatever the preference, one thing's for sure – everyone loves good homebaked cookies!

A GESTURE OF FRIENDSHIP

So you really can't go wrong if you think of cookies when it comes to gift-giving. And what a compliment it is to receive cookies as a gift. More than the most extravagant gift, homebaked cookies, specially made for you in particular, communicate caring, thought, a truly personal expression.

Cookies are appreciated any time. I bring them as house gifts, get well gifts, to parties (huge or small), celebrations and less happy gatherings. They are comforting and oftentimes reassuring.

NICE AND SIMPLE

You may want to very simply fill a plate with cookies arranged so that each kind complements the others. I always include a few colorful cookies, and look for eye appeal through varied shapes and sizes.

As I mentioned earlier, if I know someone's favorite cookies or taste preferences, then I bake that kind, and one or two others. Or I give a heaping plate filled with only the personal favorite. Cover with a heavy-duty plastic wrap, perhaps a bow or flower decoration, and you have a gift that is always appropriate, always welcome.

CREATIVE PACKAGING

There are, of course, wonderful ways to package, adorn, and enhance gift-cookies.

- Buy a small, inexpensive basket, line with a paper or cloth napkin, and gently fill with cookies. Attractive and practical, too, as cookies travel well in baskets.
- Purchase tins of varying shapes and sizes (many go on sale after Christmas, so buy then for the next year). Line tins with waxed paper and pack cookies. And don't feel limited to Christmas tins – there are many tins available with country prints or animal motifs, so you can give cookies in tins year round.
- Begin a collection of some particular item for a friend or whole family. You can package cookies together with beautiful antique cookie cutters, or butter molds, or antique napkin-rings. Every holiday and/or birthday pack cookies and another addition to the collection. A wonderfully thoughtful gift!
- Scout around garage sales, flea markets, and country auctions for interesting "cookie and" gifts. Begin to purchase antique tins, beautiful old baskets, a favorite kind of china, small salt-glazed crocks and fill them with cookies. These become treasured gifts long after the cookies are gone.
- Save your coffee tins (and their plastic tops); decorate tins with appropriate gift wrap, scraps of wallpaper or whatever is handy. Fill tins with cookies and you have a very nice gift.
- Use decorator boxes or decorate your own. Again, filled with cookies, you've created a personalized gift.

FOR SAFE KEEPING . . .

- Place waxed paper between layers of cookies.
- If packing a variety of cookies in a tin or basket, use paper cupcake liners to separate cookies – i.e., 4 *Honey-Raisin Cookies* in one liner, 4 *Chocolate Chip Crispers* in another liner, and so on. These work well for separating flavors, as well as keeping cookies from breaking.
- Always keep cookies covered to insure freshness.
- If cookies have been frozen, pack them while still frozen and even if you are visiting a neighbor, they'll be thawed before you get there. Keeps them very fresh.
- Be sure to freeze cookies you are not using immediately – they'll stay much fresher when frozen. If you will be giving them in a day or two, then refrigerate to insure freshness.
- Keep some sifted powdered sugar in a large metal salt-shaker to "refresh" cookies right before packing.
- When mailing cookies to children, friends and relatives, be sure to use good judgement. Select your least perishable recipes – those that are not delicate, frosted, or prone to melting. If you have access to the styrofoam bubbles used in packing, put some bubbles in plastic bags to line bottom and top of package. Speak to your postmaster for further advice. It's a gamble at best even with these precautions. If all fails, crumbled cookies are delicious sprinkled over a dish of ice cream.

COOKIE CATEGORIES

Cookies can fulfill special needs. That's why they are so versatile. I've listed some frequent categories along with the cookies I'd recommend to fit the need, but these are, afterall, suggestions born out of habit and personal preference.

Best to Bake With Children
Fruit Squares
Special Combination Cookies
Jewel's Cookies
Golden Nuggets
Butter Delights
Jasper Sour Cream Cookies*
Orange-Sour Cream
    Cut-Out Cookies*
Pecan Butter Balls
Chocolate Chip Cookie Bars
Poppy Seed-Lemon Cookies*
*Good for cookie cutters

Eggs-Zactly
Yolks Only
Apricot Squares (2)
Chocolate Peanut Butter
    Treasures (2)
Golden Nuggets (1)
Mocha-Nut Cookies (1)
Jewel's Cookies (2)
Chocolate Nut Meltaways (1)
Toffee Bars (1)

Whites Only
Chocolate Chip Meringue Kisses (2)
Chocolate Meringue Fluffs (3)
Date Balls (2)
Chocolate Macaroons (3)
Confetti Date Balls (2)

Fancy Cookies
Lacey Wafers
Pinwheels
Syl's Yeast Rugelah
Pecan Tarts
Bev's Shortbread Cookies
Brandy Snaps
Cream Puff Pastries
Chocolate Macaroons
Seafoam Chews
Lemony Coconut Delights
Accordion Treats
Lemon Squares
Mock Streudel
Chinese Chews
Cinnamon Crescents
Confetti Date Balls

Old-Time Favorites
Mrs. Vincent's Snickerdoodles
Ginger Snaps
Crispy Oatmeal Raisin Cookies
Famous Oatmeal Cookies
Original Toll House® Cookies
Sugar Cookies
Merlene's Hermits
Lemon Squares
Golde's Best Brownies
Mincemeat Cookies
Chocolate Chip-Peanut Butter
    Cookies

Chocolate-Lovers Heaven

Seafoam Chews
Oriental Crunch
Chocolate Chip Crispers
Golde's Best Brownies
Double-Fudge Brownies Supreme
Chocolate Meringue Fluffs
Butter Pecan Turtle Bars
Chocolate Crackles
Chocolate Peanut Butter Fantasies
Heavenly Chocolate-Nut Meltaways
Chocolate Thinsees
Chocolate Macaroons

Not Too Sweet

Coconut-Sesame Refrigerator
  Cookies
Cinnamon Crescents
Pineapple Drops
Mocha-Nut Cookies
Coffee Cookies
Cheesey Pinwheels
Accordion Treats
Honey Raisin Meltaways
Favorite Mandel Broit
Lemon-Poppy Seed Cookies

In a Hurry Cookies

Apricot Squares
Special Combination Cookies
Basic Butter Refrigerator Cookies
Butter Delights

No-Bake Rum Balls
Jewel's Cookies
Oriental Crunch

Highest Yield Cookies

Golde's Best Brownies (60)
Chocolate Meringue Fluffs (80)
Sugar Cookies (120)
Spicy Fruit Cookies (70)
Favorite Peanut Butter Cookies (95)
Original Toll House® Cookies (100)
Chocolate Crackles (96)
Ginger Snaps (84)
Brandy Snaps (100)
Mincemeat Cookies (100)
Golde's Basic Refrigerator
  Cookies (96)

Best Brunch Cookies

Honey-Zucchini Nut Bars
Spicy Applesauce Cookies
Zucchini Oatmeal Drops
Pinwheels
Mock Streudel Slices
Cinnamon Crescents
Chinese Chews
Golden Butter Tarts
Walnut Surprise
Date-Nut Squares
Cheesey Pinwheels
Accordion Treats
Pecan Pie Treasures
Favorite Mandel Broit

Index